Planet Earth The Universe's Experiment

Chris Thomas

www.capallbann.co.uk

Planet Earth The Universe's Experiment

©Copyright Chris Thomas 2003

ISBN 186163 224 X

Published by:

Capall Bann Publishing
Auton Farm
Milverton
Somerset
TA4 1NE

It is the living that need resurrecting, not the dead.

Line from a movie

By the same author:

Everything You Always Wanted To Know About Your Body, But So Far Nobody's Been Able To Tell You (with Diane Baker)

The Fools First Steps

The Healing Book (with Diane Baker)

The Journey Home

The Sequel To Everything (with Diane Baker)

D

Contents

List of Illustrations

Author's Note

We are changing.

The planet is changing.

All are searching for answers and understanding.

This is how this book came into being.

As a "psychic surgeon", I work with the consequences of these changes within peoples' bodies on an almost daily basis. With the implications of these changes comes the inevitable questions. Why is change occurring? What changes?

The answers are there and they are available to everyone but we all need guidance on how to unlock the answers we all hold. For me, I was born 'hardwired' into the section of the global mass consciousness where records are kept, a region many know as the 'Akashic'.

With direct access into these records, it was a question of how to tell the story of the Earth, its life forms and humanity as the only way to understand the current events is to place them into their correct historical context. All of the life of this Earth, with its many twists and turns, is recorded in the Akashic, sometimes in confusing detail. To bring the story of humanity to life, without confusing the reader at every point proved to be a challenge especially as most of what is recorded is totally at odds with current 'scientific' thinking and theories.

1

In the end, it was easier to follow the journey of one soul. Someone who has left a strong thread woven into the tapestry of the Earth's story.

Many ask about this character and most of the answers given rely on fantasy and myth. But all recognise some aspect of this individual's role in the history of the Earth we thought we knew.

What is the name of this character?

Merlin.

The information contained within the Akashic is totally at odds with most current scientific, archaeological and religious thinking and Merlin's role in human history is not connected with the Arthurian legend except in a consequential respect. Human history is NOT what it appears to be and our role within the entirety of life is one which we can only now begin to explore.

The subject of this book covers the whole range of human history and experience. In order to keep the book to a manageable size, I have taken an overview of events giving detail where the process of human development required further or relevant explanation. To give the whole of human history in its entirety of detail would require a work of numerous volumes and would only serve to confuse. Much of the detail is accurately covered by books written by historians and others but because of our education systems, much of the information has been misinterpreted, sometimes deliberately. This book is intended to open up the real truths behind human development and history and allow the reader to re-interpret the historical data.

There are also other forms of written work, such as channelled material, which gives areas of detail of the human process.

This book also attempts to put much of this type of material into context.

If readers require further detail of some of the references made in this book, two of my previous books, *The Journey Home* and *The Fool's First Steps* (published by Capall Bann), are available. These two books do look at some aspects of this book in greater detail.

Throughout the text there are occasional references to religious characters or religious belief systems. I do not have any religious beliefs and so these references occur only within the context of their being an aspect of human history.

Chris Thomas
December 2002

Introduction

Merlin, an enigma if ever there was one. Much has been written. Much has been said. Much has been fantasised. All from the basis of wishes and dreams.

Merlin is a reality, but one long shrouded in the recesses of the mind. How to describe a legend? How to tell his story and not have the words coloured by myth? Merlin is the Earth. Merlin is humanity. Merlin underlies all of the life on Earth. Merlin is Earth's custodian, Earth's advisor and yet Earth belongs to us all. The earth lives and breathes life into it's creations and Merlin keeps guard.

This is Merlin.

The other Merlin, well, he's the white bearded guy with a fancy cloak and staff, does magic tricks and plays with dragons. This view of Merlin is the product of the imagination of Geoffrey of Monmouth and Victorian Christian romanticism which gave us the Arthurian legend as we currently know it. The similarities between the Victorian 'Mills & Boon' and reality only lie in the names of some of the characters involved, virtually all other elements of the story are sheer fantasy.

Genealogical studies carried out by Laurence Gardner (in his book Bloodline Of The Holy Grail) show that a real Arthur did exist within history but his story is very different to that presented in the romance novels. Arthur, Gwynever, Morgain, Mordred and The Merlin all existed in reality, all sharing the same story. The real story is this:

4

The important thing to remember is the climate of the times. Britain had been under Roman occupation for some time and the Celtic clans had been pushed back into Cornwall, Wales and Scotland. Following the release from Roman rule, the clans returned to their original regions. As soon as they were settling in, the Anglo Saxons began to maraud and butcher and the Celtic clans were once again forced back into the margins of Britain.

These fragmented groups were in constant contact with each other and many intermarriages took place with family members moving from one region to another. Each region had their own princes and kings with a 'King of Kings' being appointed by a Druid council. The King of Kings was known as the Pendragon which meant the 'Head Dragon of the Island'. There is no historical Uther Pendragon. This name was invented by Geoffrey of Monmouth although uther is a Celtic word meaning 'terrible'.

Each of the regional kings had an advisor, a 'Seer to the King' who was known as 'The Merlin'. At the time of the Arthurian era the Pendragon's 'Merlin' was The Merlin Emrys of Powys who was the son of Aurelius, a high ranking Welsh druidic warrior 'priest'. Emrys succeeded as The Merlin on the death of Taliesin the Bard.

There are two historical Arthurs who held positions of 'kingship' at around the same time. The first was in Wales. This was Arthur, Prince of Dyfed who lived in the early part of the sixth century. This Arthur originally came from Leinster in Ireland and was described in the chronicles of the time as a troublesome regional interloper. Although there are many stories, and some factual records, about this Arthur, particularly in the Carmarthen and St Clears regions of Carmarthenshire and several regions of Pembrokeshire, there is no hard evidence to support the view that this is the one spoken of in legend. These speculations and misunderstandings has led to Merlin being associated with this general region of South Wales.

The other Arthur is the one of the legend.

Arthur's father was Aedan Mac Gabran of Dalriada (Western Highlands) who was appointed The Pendragon. Arthur's mother was Ygerna del Acqs (also known as Igraine) who was the true High Queen of the Celtic Kingdoms. At the time Arthur was conceived, she was still married to Gwyr - Llew the Dux (military commander) of Carlisle. Aedan and Ygerna married on Gwyr - Llew's death and legitimised Arthur's title. Arthur became Pendragon when his father was appointed King of Scots.

Arthur married Gwenhwyfer of Brittany but they had no children. However, Arthur did father one son by his sister Morgaine (also known as Morganna and Morgan le faye) and he was called Mordred.

Fathering children with your sister sounds incestuous to us but it was a common practice expected of kingly blood lines where both male and female sides of the blood lines were seen as equally valid. Within the Druidic traditions such matings would take place at Beltane. These traditions were eventually stopped, and made a sin, by the Catholic Church when they forcibly took control of appointing kings. With this tradition made a sin, the Catholic Church could take control of and disrupt ancient blood lines who were a potential threat to the power of the church.

Morgaine married King Urien of Rheged and Gowrie. Morgaine was a Celtic High Priestess and held the title of Holy Sister of Avalon.

The whole story centres around Carlisle which was then called Cardeol or Caruele which was the provincial capitol.

6

There was a 'Camelot', actually Camulod, which was a Celtic name meaning 'curved light'. This Camulod was modern day Colchester, the greatest Iron Age fort in Britain, and is where Boudicca (Boadicea) was based around AD 60.

Arthur's family were Celtic Christians which was a blend of the true teachings of Jesus with that of Druidic beliefs (see chapters seven and nine). Arthur became attracted to the Roman Catholic version of Christianity which was an opposing view to the true Druidic teachings and began to use his army as 'Holy Crusaders' to bring Roman beliefs to Scotland. His son, Mordred, was High Priest of the Celtic Church and although Arthur held the title of Defender of the Faith, Mordred held a higher spiritual office. This placed father and son on opposing sides. Most of the Celts supported Mordred as they saw Roman Christianity as a major threat to their traditions and chosen way of life and so the Celtic kings rose up against Arthur.

A King Aethelfrith gathered together an army to oppose Arthur which led to battles at Camlanna (near Hadrian's Wall) and Dawston-on-Solway where both Arthur and Mordred were killed on opposing sides. Had Mordred survived the battle, he would have become Pendragon and Britain's history would probably have been very different. With both Arthur and Mordred dead, it broke up the Celtic clans and no new leader arose who could reunite them.

In Geoffrey of Monmouth's version of events (written in 1147), the whole story has been moved to Glastonbury and Tintagel to suit the political aspirations of the local land owner who sponsored Geoffrey to write the story. The roles of Arthur and Mordred have also been reversed, with Arthur now as the hero instead of someone who turned against his own people. By the time Geoffrey of Monmouth wrote his story, Britain was Roman Catholic and as Arthur had tried to impose Roman Christianity on the Celts, he was cast as the hero.

Mordred had to be cast as the villain as he had defended the Celtic Christian beliefs against the Romanised version. Merlin took on the role of the 'wicked sorcerer' who disappeared when Roman Catholicism took over and defeated Druidic beliefs.

The Victorians were very keen on the romantic version of events and Geoffrey of Monmouth's stories were further embellished to arrive at the version of the Arthurian legend we know today.

The real Merlin was not involved in this page of history, but his name has been unfortunately linked with the romance and our understanding of the true role he has played has become lost. This book is an attempt to re-find Merlin.

The story told here is not a romance. It is the history of the Earth, and all of its life, as recorded in the mass consciousness. In its original form, the planetary consciousness held the whole of our history but as humanity developed, their mass consciousness came into being as a separate, but interrelated, form of memory. The human mass consciousness also contains the memories of its origins and its struggles. These two forms of consciousness, the planet and humanity, touch and combine in the deepest regions of the human consciousness and this combined record has been traditionally known as The Akashic Records. The word 'Akashic' is Sumerian and means 'record'.

Related in this book is a journey through The Akashic.

Chapter One

Before Time

All things have a beginning.

This universe, like all of the other nine, began with a thought. The thought is freedom of choice. This thought has determined, and continues to determine all of the activities that take place within this universe - total freedom of choice. This freedom extends to all life, from the universal consciousness itself all the way down to the simplest form of life. The only limiting factor is the individual's awareness of the reality that the choice exists.

The first phase of this universe's choice lasted 395 000 million years and its choice was to start again.

All of the life that formed that first attempt decided to make a fresh start but with a greater understanding of the way in which choice, and total freedom, can work. It is difficult to know what to do when your opportunities and possibilities are limitless. The other universes all explore a theme, an aspect of a thought, whereas ours has no limits.

To begin a universe, the 'fields of possibility' that are our "Creator" combine together to form a new frequency for life. All life is energy and each frequency of that energy combines to mould and determine the whole. Each frequency of that energy has a purpose and a function and it is the combining of a particular range of frequencies that determines the "theme" that each universe is capable of exploring. The other universes all have limits, a predetermined range of frequencies that limits the range of activities that can take place. In our universe, the full range of possible frequencies are present and, therefore, all potential exists.

From our perspective, that of humanity, the vastness of this limitless possibility is a concept almost impossible to grasp. How can we, in our limited shells, understand the vastness of no limit? The time is rapidly approaching when we will, but for now, it is no more than an unrealised, and barely understood, concept.

All things have a beginning

Our universe began 475 000 000 000 (four hundred and seventy five thousand million) years ago with the formation of an "envelope" of energy that contains all of the range of energy frequencies that are required for a total freedom of choice. A limitless potential.

The universe looks very much like the images we have of galaxies. From the top, a circular swirl, or vortex spiral. From the side, a central flat plane which rises from its edges to form a central dome both above and below the centre.

Within this "envelope" the first act of awareness begins with the formation of the universal consciousness. This consciousness, or awareness, is made up of thirteen elements, each performing an aspect of the work required to maintain the universal balance of energies. Although each of the thirteen could be viewed as a separate being in their own right, it is probably easier to think of them as a combined consciousness that acts as one.

Once the universal "being" is formed, other acts of creation (coming into existence) take place.

All life is aware of itself, to one degree or another, and aware of the potential that is contained within the self. That potential is reflected by the range and magnitude of energy frequencies contained within that individual.

The first "life" to form are those which contain the greatest potential for life and therefore, the greatest range of energy potential. These are the lesser "universes" we know as galaxies. Once these galaxies are formed, the situation starts to become more complicated.

Universal Consciousness

All life is formed by an individual dividing into more than one. For example, the Creator exists in a realm where all energies and, therefore, all possibilities exist. The generation of a life (consciousness) separate from those possibilities requires an act of "creation". Once that new, individual consciousness has been formed, it also has the capability of creating further life. This is how all beings are brought into existence. Therefore, the possibility exists for the generation of new life from two sources. The first is directly from "source" and the second is from a consciousness already created.

Most life within our universe is actually generated by the universal consciousness making use of its own energy potential.

Once the galactic structures are in place, other levels of consciousness begin to form. These are the stars, or suns. Stars are formed by either of two processes. The first is by the galactic consciousness forming a separate, but fully connected, part of itself into a new consciousness. The second is by the universal consciousness bringing about a star within the galactic envelope. This is only achieved with the full co-operation of the galactic being - collective free choice.

This is how the universe remained for many millions of years - a relatively small number of galaxies and stars exploring the possibilities offered by this level of existence. This process still continues today. New galaxies and new stars form at a time appropriate to the individual consciousness that makes up the new formation. In this way, the universe always appears to be expanding. All that is really occurring is individuals are fulfilling their potential at a time which is of their choosing. This means that the universe is always developing, exploring new possibilities, during its total existence.

As humans, most of us have some difficulty in grasping this concept. We have become used to seeing the space around us as being composed of "dead" matter. Our materialistic world only allows for the possibility of material things and we have, largely, forgotten about the underlying energies that comprises all of the matter we consider "dead". If we take a look at the shape of the universe it can, perhaps, make this concept easier to understand.

The universe is shaped like a circle made up of swirling vortices of the limitless energy potential that the universe has as its range of possibilities. Within this potential is an inherent knowledge and awareness of itself (consciousness).

Galaxies are formed of swirling vortices of vast energy potential which that galaxy has as its range of possibilities. Within this potential is an inherent knowledge and awareness of itself. All matter is composed of swirling vortices of energy potential that combine together to form all matter (the atoms of which all matter is comprised). Within that swirl of energies is the potential to be aware of itself. But, when we reduce the energy potential down to an atomic level, the energetic building blocks of matter, it only has the possibility of awareness and it needs to be combined with others of similar potential to reach a level where awareness can be realised. It is other, higher, levels of awareness that bring

12

together these smaller vortices and give them life. In other words, a conscious energy combines together a number of these atoms to share its energy with that of the atoms, producing "physical" matter. It is the unaware energy potential of an atom that provides the raw material from which all structure is formed.

This was the next stage of development within the universe. The aware beings that form stars make use of their own potential to form a smaller being using the energy of the freely available atoms to generate a structure with a greater density. In other words, a planet.

Planets are formed by a star as an element of the star's consciousness. This particular consciousness decides to make use of its own potential to generate a new part of itself. As it projects this element of itself into a new location, it draws upon the freely available energies which exist in all regions of the universe. The new planetary consciousness is shaped like the universe, or a galaxy, and it begins to spin at a higher speed.

All energy spins and takes the form of a vortex. The higher the energy potential, the slower the spin. This is the reason why the universe revolves at one speed, the galaxies a little faster, stars a little faster still, planets much faster than their suns and atoms spin at comparatively high speeds.

So, there now existed a universe inhabited with a small number of galaxies, suns and planets. This does not mean that we would necessarily recognise them as such. Stars and planets at this stage in universal development were still at very high frequencies of energy. This means that they did not have much in the way of physical density.

As part of their own potential, planets can also generate their own forms of life. These forms of life take shape in the flora and fauna of that planet. As each planet is an individual, each expresses those forms of life in their own way, leading to a very high diversity of forms of life throughout the universe.

Onto these newly formed worlds a more mobile form of life was reintroduced (from the first universal attempt). These new forms were not generated by any of the galaxies or stars, not even by the universal consciousness, but by the fields of possibility that we call The Creator.

These six different forms of life formed the first six "civilisations" within this universe and came into being roughly twenty-eight million years ago. These six civilisations we know collectively as "Angels" and their part in human history is chronicled in "The Fool's First Steps".

Several further stages of development of suitable life forms then ensued. All of these stages resulted in the creation of free thinking, free acting and free choosing totally independent forms of life. They all fulfilled the Creator's wish for the life of this universe: total freedom of choice.

Other Forms of Universal Life

The first 'creationary' act is to bring into being those who will maintain the balance of energies to bring the universal thought to fruition. These 'balancers', a management, is comprised of thirteen beings. These thirteen form a collective who take charge of the universe in the role of guardians of the thought.

These thirteen balance and weigh all choices and all available energies to maintain the balance of energies. They are also co creators of the universe in that they can bring about forms of life which they consider will enhance the universe's explorations. It is the Thirteen who create plant and animal forms and imbue them with consciousness but it is the

Creator, and only the Creator, who creates higher consciousness forms.

The Thirteen Civilisations

Within our universe, there are thirteen 'civilisations'.

The first to be created are entirely non physical. There are six
of these civilisations.

Each was brought into being in very different regions of the
universe and each took very many millions of years to
understand themselves and their place within the universe.
Eventually, these different civilisations came together and
now form a cohesive group. Collectively, these six civilisations
are what we would currently call 'The Angels' - more about
that later.

These six civilisations exist in all regions of the universe and
assist all life in its choices and the struggles brought about by
those choices. They also work very closely with the Thirteen.

This is the second time that this universe has been formed. If
you have absolute freedom to choose, how do you make
choices without understanding where those choices can take
you. Collectively, our choice the first time around was to start
again.

Some physical density was experimented with as part of our
first attempt and with our choice to start again, came the
beginnings of the exercise of choice to explore physical
density. The six 'higher' civilisations are entirely non physical.
This means that they exist in a state of pure energy. They are
called 'higher' only in the sense that they have no physical
form and does not imply any kind of superiority over the other
races. Physical density was unknown to them. As a fundamental part of the choice to start again was the wish to

explore what it means to be physical and so the 'experiment' of Earth was planned right at the very beginning, however, in order to begin to understand something of the potential complexities of this state of being, beings who are semi physical were planned to explore the intermediary stage.

There are seven semi physical 'civilisations' within this universe all at various stages of development and various levels of density. The order in which they are given here is to do with the amount of interaction they have had with Earth and does not suggest a 'hierarchy' of any kind.

NGC 584

The first group are the ones who have worked with the Earth for the longest period. Their home worlds, what could be described as their 'soul origins', does not have a name, just an astronomers' catalogue number, NGC 584.

The NGC are the universes' master geneticists, they hold a record of all of the life that has ever existed within this universe and are capable of reproducing any of their stored DNA back into physical form. For example, when we have completed our transitions and brought the planet back to its original pristine condition, we could reintroduce the Dodo, or any other species man has made extinct.

Their home world has an average temperature of minus 200 centigrade which makes it perfect for the storage of genetic material. They average about two foot six (75cm) in height and look a little like a human two year old but with a rusty red and bluish grey skin.

They first began working with Earth about twenty million years ago where they assisted the planet to design and construct the first life forms on Earth. They have worked with the Earth ever since. When Merlin and the Lady began the reconstruction process following the destruction of Atlantis, it was to these individuals they turned to for advice and assistance (see chapter four).

They act with immense integrity. The human scientists' concept of tinkering just for profit does not enter into their minds as they have no need for material gain.

It should also be remembered that as a soul within this universe, we have absolute free choice and where there are compatible energies, a soul can exist in any 'physical' form. In this way there are currently ninety eight thousand NGC's in human form on the planet. They are also, in their natural form, helping us through our integration by monitoring our genetic changes.

Pleiadeans
The next group are more well known, these are those souls who originated on a star system we have called the Pleiades. Our other names for this star system are The Seven Sisters and 'Little Eyes'.

On their home world the Pleiadeans are between seven and eight foot tall (2 - 2.5m), very slim with an elegant 'human' form. They appear to have an inner glow of energy that makes them look almost translucent.

Like the NGC, Pleiadeans have an immense integrity which means that they will not take any actions to deliberately harm.

Many Pleiadeans were on Atlantis to discover the pleasures of full physical life and have remained working with humanity and the planet ever since. These peoples are also insatiable travellers and have lived many lifetimes on many different worlds either in their original form or in the form of the fully conscious life of the planet. They have also spread out far and wide throughout the universe and have colonised a large number of worlds.

They are currently undergoing their own transitionary process where they will lose all of their physical density and revert to a pure energy form.

They communicate with complex thought wave patterns which they have also used to communicate with some human channels. Their communications have not been wrong in the past but as they do not have full information on how humanity is developing, some of their communications have been a little wide of the mark as they have seen possibilities which were not necessarily the best direction for us to travel in.

They wish to visit us in their natural form to try to help us with our transitions. They see a visit by them as a way of breaking some of the stereotypical ideas we have adopted over the centuries. Unfortunately, their efforts to visit have been thwarted by the American military.

There are currently one hundred and eight thousand living in human form on Earth.

Sirians

The next group come from a star system we have called Sirius, the Dog Star.

The Sirians are four foot six (1.4m) in height and look like a smaller version of us. They do not have any hair, have large eyes and are pale skinned which has a slightly green cast.

They have not had a great deal of involvement in human development although some aspects of their DNA structures were used to help Cro Magnon development into Homo Sapien Sapien. As we have developed from this source we do carry some genetic memories of this time and this is why Sirius appears very familiar to many.

They have great difficulty transferring from their natural form into human form and so only twelve thousand seven hundred and sixty are in human form on the planet.

They also communicate psychically and have communicated with many on Earth. The problem with these communications is that whilst the core of their messages is true, they tend to embroider most of the facts and this is why so many of their communications have not been strictly accurate.

They also wish to see humanity complete their transition and have provided energy 'transformers' to modulate the new energies entering our region of space to suit our various stages in development. These transformers are large black monoliths, a little like the one in Stanley Kubrick's movie *2001 A Space Odyssey*. A number of astronomers and astronauts have reported sightings of these monoliths within the solar system.

Greys

The next group are those which UFO watchers have christened the 'Greys'. These tend to be about three foot six (1.1m) in height and have a grey, smooth skin. They have no discernible facial features other than their very large and very black eyes. Their eyes are not actually black but are 'reptilian' with a vertical iris. The blackness of their eyes comes from the fact that they are subterranean dwellers on their home world and wear eye shields when in direct light.

They live in a region of space which we have not charted and so we do not have a name, or even a number, for their home star system. This group, along with the one listed below, are responsible for the vast majority of UFO sightings and abductions that take place on the planet. They are a little like teenagers in that they have a great deal of knowledge but do not yet fully understand the consequences of their actions. The primary reason for the abductions is in order for them to develop a human form that they could inhabit. In other words, become more human in appearance. What they took a long time to realise is that the physical form follows the form of the soul and it is therefore not very easy to modify their physical form that radically.

Their preferred source of food is emotional energy which they have found in abundance on Earth. It is in their own interests to keep humanity from developing as they would lose this food source. They have carried out some abductions to try to increase our sense of unease and panic. However, their main strategy to feed themselves, in the last sixty years, has been to take on a disguise and pass themselves off to various human groups as 'Ascended Masters'. Within the Akashic, there is no meaning ascribed to this term and it was coined by humans to salve their egos. Can we really blame the Greys for taking advantage of a situation some members of human society brought upon themselves?

Some people, who work as channellers, have reported working with beings of this appearance but they have felt that the ones they are working with act with integrity and without any attempt to coerce or mislead. The physical appearances of greys can be confused with that of those of Sirian origin and this is where the confusion can arise. Always ensure that if you carry out any channelling work that you are working with those of the highest integrity and motives. Always ask questions.

All of the Greys, ascended masters or otherwise, have now been removed from our solar system and their means of access, the Draco gate has been shut to them (see illustration one).

Blues

There is a group who travel quite frequently with the greys and UFO watchers have christened them the 'Blues' because of their appearance.

These beings are about three feet (1m) tall and fairly round in shape with short legs. Their heads and bodies are covered in short, dark blue hair.

They too originate in a region of space uncharted by us.

The Blues and Greys usually travel together and the Blues have developed an extremely high knowledge of genetics and genetic manipulation although not as advanced as the NGC nor, sadly, do they have their ethics and integrity although they are beginning to learn. Like the Greys, their access to this solar system has now been denied.

Unnamed Civilisations

Another group has only begun to explore the regions outside of their own galaxy in recent years and so their visits to earth have been very infrequent and tend not to last very long as their senses cannot deal with the amount and volume of sounds we make.

They are about eight feet (2.4m) tall with large bodies and comparatively small heads. They tend to wear full environment suits, when away from their home worlds, which are made of a fabric that looks a little like blue tin foil.

Again, their home region is too remote for us to have charted.

They have not had any involvement with the Earth or humanity but would like to return to visit when our transitions are complete.

The final group of the seven 'lower' civilisations lives on the other side of the universe to us. Their physical structures are based upon silica and so look like crystal and rock formations. Their levels of consciousness are exceptionally advanced and they look forward to a visit from us sometime.

These are the thirteen civilisations which comprise conscious life within our universe. Despite its immense size, the universe is not always an empty place. The Six Higher Civilisations inhabit and can readily travel to all regions and many have taken up residence on a huge variety of worlds. The Seven Lower Civilisations also occupy many worlds both in this galaxy and in others and very many worlds have developed and are developing an unbelievable variety of plant and animal forms.

There are, however, two other forms of life which we have not yet mentioned and both live in our solar system.

Other Life Forms

Jupiter is a planet that was dramatically affected by the self destruction of the two planets that exploded within our solar system (see The Beginnings of Life later in this chapter). It went from a world of life to a gas giant which is potentially turning into a second sun. Of its thirteen moons, one harbours fully conscious life. This is Gannymede.

Gannymede is a little smaller than Earth and is covered in a two mile thickness of ice. Under the ice, there is a great deal of volcanic activity and like the black smokers in Earth's deep oceans, there are sufficient nutrients to support life.

These beings are a development of the life which originally inhabited Venus, that is, a little like a dolphin in form but with enlarged front limbs and their skin is like a snake's skin. On Venus they were truly amphibian and lived in both the vast seas and forest covered lands.

On Gannymede, they have adapted to life under water and live on the smaller life that is nourished by the nutrients supplied by deep volcanic vents.

They too are waiting for us to reach their level of understanding and will not show themselves until humanity does so.

The Birth of Humanity

With the success of the seven 'lower' or semi physical races, the universal consciousness decided that a new form of life could be attempted. Life at the proposed level of existence had never been tried before and so it was begun with a certain degree of trepidation but also excitement.

The idea was to bring about a fully aware being which was constructed of a highly compacted energy. The six civilisations, for example, were formed of very high frequency energy. This meant that they have a body form but no body density. To us, they look transparent but human in shape. These new beings were to be of the same high frequency as the six but were to have a physical form that has an extremely high density. A high level of conscious awareness but contained within a fully "physical" body.

This had never been tried before - anywhere. No other universe had beings of this form who were also of this high an awareness and special precautions needed to be taken to ensure there would not be any major problems.

A new process began. The idea had first been formulated during the first phase of universal development and, at the beginning of the second phase, the initial stages of those plans were begun. The first step was to find a star who would be prepared to take part in such an unusual "experiment". One was found on the outer edge of a large galaxy near the edge of the universal envelope. Once the star was prepared, an energy "envelope" was created which would contain this region of space. A miniature, self contained "universe".

Within the universal void, the spaces between the galaxies, energy is infinite. If travelling through the universe, speeds are also at infinity. In other words, although there is space between the galaxies, the time taken to travel from one galaxy to another is zero. Energy condenses and slows the closer a traveller passes by a galaxy. Within the galaxies themselves, energy (and, therefore, space and the speed of light) varies depending upon the needs and choices of the consciousness that formed that galaxy. The energy is again adjusted by the individual stars and star systems, of which the galaxy is comprised, to suit their own needs and choices.

A similar process was undergone in this new envelope. Energy was condensed to an almost infinite degree. This had the effect of slowing down all of the processes and energies that were to be contained around this star system.

Into this envelope there were introduced thirteen independent beings. These conscious beings wrapped around themselves these dense energies and formed thirteen totally individual planets that worked with, but were not a part of, the star's consciousness. This was also very unusual. Galaxies form stars or invite stars to inhabit their "space". These stars then form planets as part of their own plans and choices.

In our star system, the planets are individuals within their own right. This idea was chosen as the best course of action in order to maximise potential and creativity.

The effect of this "envelope" was two fold. The first was to contain the new energy potentials that were necessary for the formation of these planets and the planned life forms and, secondly, to prevent the universal energies seeping into the star system and disrupting the "experiment".

It is this envelope and the range of energy frequencies contained within it which give us our form and density, even so, it still contains an energy potential of 293 dimensions. Nowhere else, in the whole of creation, does life exist at such an energy combination. Once the thirteen planetary consciousness' had completed their planet building tasks, the next phase was begun.

Each of the thirteen planets began to develop life and each planet was helped to develop this life by transporting forms of life from other worlds. The choice of life forms depended upon their adaptability to energies of an extremely high density. They were also chosen for their abilities to transform and generate suitable atmospheres, a different blend of gases and life supporting other substances as each planet required. On Earth, plants were formed which could carry out this task and the process of life generation began a little over 20 million years ago. The scientific world considers dates and time periods much older than this but that is to misread and misunderstand the stories the rocks have to tell. With this process begun, all of these planets were left to their own devices for several million years.

When each planet felt it was ready, a new phase began. This was to introduce forms of life which had the potential to develop into beings which could reach a full state of conscious awareness. It was necessary to introduce species of this type as the planetary consciousness' were only capable of generating forms of life which shared with their own

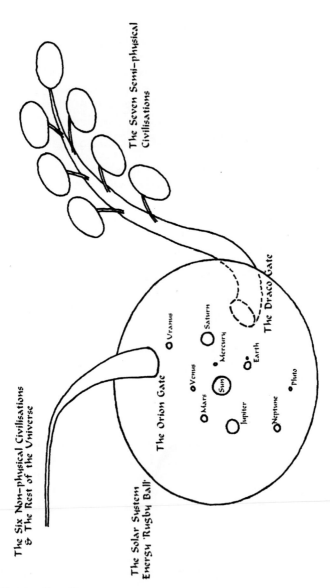

The Seven Semi-physical
Civilisations

The Draco Gate

Uranus

Saturn

Mercury

Earth

Venus

Sun

Mars

Jupiter

Neptune

Pluto

The Orion Gate

The Six Non-physical Civilisations
& The Rest of the Universe

The Solar System
Energy 'Rugby Ball'

Illustration One
The Solar System Energy Envelope

consciousness. In this way, all of the plants and animals that live on a planet are a part of that planet's own being and form what could be described as a "group soul".

The process is, basically, this. The planetary consciousness decides on the type of life forms that it would like to bring into being. In order to achieve this, it generates an energy field which has the form of the plant or animal. This is the "etheric template" for that animal or plant type - a form of energy blueprint. This energy framework is then copied to form individual members of a particular group. Each individual then uses the raw materials available on the planet to give itself form and matter. Although it is an individual plant or animal, it remains a part of its respective group soul and, therefore, a part of the planet's own consciousness.

In order to generate free thinking and free acting beings, the planetary consciousness has to decide between two choices.

First, does it generate such sentient beings and very little in the way of plants and animals? A star or planet only contains a limited range of energy frequencies and cannot generate an infinite variety of life. Within our solar system, this choice was even more limited by the density of the available energies.

Secondly, does it create as much diversity as possible and allow other beings to inhabit it? In the case of these thirteen planets, the second choice was more appropriate. This choice allowed for a greater level of experimentation to take place. Life at this level of existence had never been attempted before and it was decided, collectively, to explore as many forms of life as possible. Before this final stage could occur, an intermediate development needed to be tried to decide on the physical scale of the final inhabitants.

There could not be any way of predetermining the effects of high density energy on levels of awareness and so the planets of the universe were explored to find as large a range of suitable forms of life as possible. All of these life forms had to be capable of adaption to the solar system's high density and variety of life supporting atmospheres. All thirteen planets were newly seeded in this way and life developed at an amazing pace. It soon became very obvious that life of all shapes and sizes could adapt to our peculiar environments and a choice had to be made to find the most suitable size to progress with the overall plan.

Once these decisions had been made and the final form of the experiment had been determined, each planet was given a "guardian".

The Creation of Merlin

The thirteen beings, of which the universal consciousness is formed, are able to create life. This is, after all, a major part of their primary function. In order to fulfil their creationary role, each of the thirteen "breaks off" a piece of itself and forms a new individual. Thirteen of these "guardians" were created in this way. Each of these advisors were a product of the collective will of all of the thirteen. The thirteen beings used their collective mind to create these thirteen guardians. This meant that each of these guardians shared aspects of all of the thirteen beings. Each of these guardians were given a planet to work with.

In the case of Earth, our guardian became known as Merlin. Merlin was born of this universe and his role is to work with our planet and with humanity to maximise potential and to ensure that freedom of choice is maintained. Four million years ago, Merlin began his work with Earth and humanity.

The History of the Earth

To place this story into its full context, we need to dig deeper into history and extend our search to include the planet itself. In order to access this aspect of the Akashic, it is a matter of extending our search deeper into the mass consciousness and travel through to contact the consciousness of the planet itself. Most of the information to be found there is at complete odds with the scientific view of the world, its time frame and the sequence of events. There is something strange about the way we humans go about looking at ourselves and the world around us. The ones who have set themselves up as investigators of the truth, the scientists, have always maintained remarkably closed minds. Instead of thinking about their findings or the hints given to them by the rocks, they have consistently chosen assumption and arrogance over truth with the picture even further distorted by an adherence to man made religions.

The truth is not hard to find, it just requires a little perseverance and an open mind.

The planet is a consciousness. It came to be in our region of space to take part in an experiment with life. Our sun was the first life to arrive in this region of space and chose to light a solar system that was not yet formed but provided the initial potential for other life to follow. Once the sun had begun to develop, the other living beings arrived in a slow procession until the thirteen planets had formed. As they arrived, the planets set about forming themselves into platforms where other life could be created and develop. Three hundred and forty seven million years ago, the solar system was complete.

In order to facilitate the forming of the solar system, energy was made available from the universal energy structures and our whole region of space was contained within an energy 'bubble' which would provide energies of a blend of frequencies which would serve to assist in the formation of 'physical' life and maintain its physical density. This envelope is shaped a little like a rugby ball and contains a total energy potential of 293 dimensions.

Into this 'rugby ball' of space there are two 'gateways'. One connects to the universal void, and therefore its limitless energies, and is through the constellation of Orion. The second 'gateway' connects into the energies of the semi physical life forms of the universe, the seven lower civilisations, and is through the constellation of Draco. It is through this Draco gate that all of the early forms of life in the solar system came.
Not all life began developing at the same time. Each planet had its own process and own enthusiasm for the work to come and so developed suitable habitats in their own way and in their own time. On Earth, the full work began a little over twenty five million years ago.

The Earth began its life with a much smaller diameter. Its diameter was approximately 54% of what it currently is. This was a process of development from its origins as a "lifeless" rock to a life supporting planet. The expansion has occurred as the planet's energies altered and expanded to receive its anticipated inhabitants. Once it had coalesced and transmuted sufficient energy to receive life, it was about 75% of its current diameter.

The scientific view of a single land mass, Pangea, never occurred. All of the land masses, with the exception of South America and the continent of Atlantis, were in more or less their current positions. Plate tectonics have played no part in shaping our world, it has been formed by the expansion of the soul that is the Earth and one near catastrophic event.

The scientific evidence for internal expansion and not plate tectonic movement comes from two directions.

The actual pattern of rock formations around deep sea trenches shows that over millions of years there has been expansion, not displacing movement bringing about continental drift. This is further evidenced by the volume and pattern of river deposits on the fringes of the continents.

For plate tectonics to be a viable theory, the Pacific ocean must shrink every year to accommodate the continued movements to allow for continental drift (plate subduction). The Pacific shrinkage needs to be in the region of 20mm per year and takes place through subduction zones at its edges. Current satellite measurements, through the Global Positioning System (GPS) shows that the Pacific is actually expanding at the rate of about 19mm per year.

This is not the whole story as there is also memory of periods of contraction which account for some of the fluctuations in water levels and we will explore these memories a little later.

The Beginnings of Life

Life began with bacteria and a judicious dollop of slime (algae). The bacteria to generate suitable atmospheric gases and the algae to provide the raw materials for plants. With the arrival of life, guardians were needed to assist, develop, create and nurture and so the planet brought forth the first of its own creationary forms, the Sidhé and the faerie. For twenty million years the Sidhé and the faerie have been the 'gardeners' of our world and it is now time to feel their full influence again.

The Sidhé (pronounced Shee) exist in a pure energy form which feeds off the planet's own energy emissions and so do not require 'food' beyond this. Their work began with the design and construction of suitable plant forms to be a food source for the animals and fish that were to come. The work was begun using designs of plants on other worlds which were supplied by the inhabitants of NGC 584. These energy components, etheric fields, were brought through the Draco gate and began to take on density as soon as they entered our solar system envelope.

With these plants in place, work on others began, some were modifications to the ones introduced whilst most were new. As the population of plants grew, the Faerie were brought into being to act as the world's 'gardeners'. The Faerie do eat their plants but in an energetic form that is somewhere between the material form and the etheric form.

With a changing atmosphere and a growing plant source for food it was seen as a suitable time to introduce animal life. The first were introduced into the seas. The problem with this solar system is that life forms of a physical density of this nature had not been generated in any part of the universe before and there were concerns about the effects of gravity upon internal organs. For this reason the seas were seeded with life first as the pressure of the water could counteract the effects of gravity.

Everything began small. Nobody knew how the intense gravity and physical structures would affect this life - it had never been attempted before. As success followed success, more and larger species were introduced.

When it came to the land, the process of introduction was again slow and cautious. Would these animals adapt? Could the plant species already developed support life? Would the plants themselves survive? Nobody knew.

This is how life on Earth continued for several million years. Experimentation, creation and evolution. All added knowledge and understanding and with the growing level of understanding came further developments.

After about five million years the Earth and its life had stabilised. The atmosphere was more or less as it is now except with a higher percentage of carbon dioxide. Many plants and animals had developed into larger and higher forms and were beginning to thrive. There were two basic groups, reptile and mammal although the largest of the two groups were reptiles. The Sidhé took on responsibility for all forms of life at this stage and it was they who maintained and developed the etheric templates of all life.

With this stability it was decided to experiment a little more with new life and a highbrid form of these two animal types were slowly developed. These we know as the dinosaurs. They were not truly reptile neither were they mammal. The reason for their immense size stemmed from the primary purpose of the Earth experiment, a physical structure robust enough and developed enough to accommodate a full individual consciousness, a full individual soul.

Animals, fish, birds and plants have a group soul, one soul 'pattern' for each species. It was hoped that one of the developing variety on Earth would evolve into a form which could develop into an individual. A being that could act as a true individual not dependant upon a group consciousness. Many variations were tried. Were the ones who lived in water better? Were the ones on land? If so, mammals or reptiles? Hybrids? Did size matter? Nobody knew.

Throughout this universe the higher forms of life, the thirteen civilisations, were all of a basic humanoid form. On Earth it was decided to try to find out if an alternative form was possible. Was one of the wide diversity of life forms capable of evolution into a sentient being? Everything had to be tried.

Eventually, it became clear that a primate form was exhibiting the most promising developments. All other life forms were very slow to develop and were not evolving in directions which made it look as though a non humanoid form was possible. Four and a half million years ago, a group of primates took the first steps towards becoming Neanderthal man.

This move was very encouraging but Earth was a planet of a level of abundance of life which had never been thought possible. Was there room on this world for the primates to evolve naturally? Many of the animal species on land, sea and air were predatory and posed a direct threat to primate, pre human, existence. If a being capable of taking on full consciousness was to develop from these primates then it would be prudent to remove some of the most dangerous species.

The Sidhé and the planet began to work on this problem and set into motion a reversal of the evolution process for some of the most dangerous types of predators. This was meant to be a gentle process which would take several thousands of years to fulfil.

At this point, a disaster occurred which was so catastrophic that the whole venture was almost abandoned.

The solar system had thirteen planets each of which developed its own forms of life unique to the consciousness of the planet. Some developed along similar lines but most were totally original.

About four and a half million years ago four of the planets decided that they could not sustain their existence and two of the consciousnesses removed themselves from the 'rock' of their planet.

This kind of event occurs fairly commonly throughout the universe, the planetary consciousness leaves its constructed shell and the energy of the shell, the planet itself, dissipates and is used by other planets or stars for their own raw material needs. With our solar system events occurred a little differently. Instead of the energies of the 'rock' dissipating, it exploded. The density of the energies comprising the planet's shell were such that the removal of the consciousness produced a massive explosion. The material took off with such force that it ripped through the solar system causing catastrophic damage. All life was wiped out on all of the planets with the exception of Earth and Jupiter's moon, Gannymede.

The Earth gained a moon as a fragment of one of these planets and most of Earth's atmosphere was ripped away. The planet was violently rocked on its equatorial axis and most life, and especially the dinosaurs, were destroyed.

The other residue from these two planets form the asteroid belts between Saturn and Jupiter and outside Uranus.

The other two planets who wished to leave the solar system were helped to leave 'whole' before the planetary consciousness cast off their shells and the residual material could explode without harm. It was at this point, four million years ago, that Merlin first came to Earth.

The arrival of the Planetary Guardians

All thirteen of the planets in our solar system were given a guardian by the universal consciousness and each of the thirteen guardians arrived at different times to suit the stage of development appropriate to each planet. Each planet developing at its own pace and in its own way. As the emergence of a life form capable of evolving into a conscious being occurred, the guardian was despatched to their appropriate planet. In this process Merlin was the last to arrive as Earth was the last planet to develop.

Merlin's first task was to work with the Sidhé and the planet to rebuild. A great deal had been lost and much was needed to be done. His second task was to introduce life forms from some of the worlds who no longer sustained life. The primary task was to bring in the humanoid form that had been developing on Mars. We know these new arrivals as Cro Magnon Man.

With the beginnings of the work with the two potential human groups, Neanderthal Man and Cro Magnon Man, the Earth began a new period of expansion and its diameter slowly enlarged. By the time Atlantis was established, 85 000 years ago, the planet's diameter was ten percent larger than it is now. As Atlantis developed (see Chapter Two), the planet continued to grow and by 75 000 years ago it was about thirty percent larger than it currently is. This meant that sea level was about two hundred foot lower than present.

With the destruction of Atlantis, the planet underwent a rapid shrinkage to about ninety percent of its present size. This rapid shrinkage brought about the surface changes that were experienced at the time. The Rising of the Alps, the formation of the Himalayas etc. were all brought about by this shrinking. The sea level rose by about three hundred foot and many lands were flooded.

The whole topography of the planet changed. As the planet underwent its axis shift, the polar ice caps formed reducing the new sea level down to its present levels.

The planet has remained fairly stable since then with only the occasional earthquake shaking its surface. As humanity underwent its knowledge gathering processes, our interaction with the Earth has diminished and the planetary consciousness has rarely stirred. With the coming of the twentieth century and as humanity began to rise to the completion of the Karmic process, the planetary consciousness

36

has begun to move with us. The more that we change, the more the planet begins to expand. This is where most of the glacier and ice cap melt water has been accommodated, the planet is once again expanding.

It is very sad to note that several groups are working globally to halt earthquakes occurring. What is not realised is that earthquakes are occurring as a result of the Earth's expansion. Working to prevent these growing pains is having two effects. The first is it is slowing down the planet's ability to move and work with us. The second is that where earthquakes do occur they are more severe and damaging than if the Earth was allowed to move in its own way.

As humanity undergoes its final clearance and soul integration, the planet will continue to expand and change the atmosphere to what they were at the middle of the Atlantis period. This time, hopefully, mankind will be able to maintain its level of consciousness and the Earth will once again be working with us to maintain the physical paradise the Earth truly is.

Chapter Two
Before Atlantis

The loss of the four planets was catastrophic as far as the solar system was concerned. The remaining nine planets were all severely affected by this change and most of the life on these planets was lost. Earth was very nearly destroyed and it was only with the planetary consciousness' determination to continue that Earth's new 'Guardian', Merlin, was able to help to bring stability back to this part of space.

When the dust finally settled, a new start was made and the first steps towards the full development of humanity were taken.

Earth renewed.

Earth Begun.

Humanity's dawn.

The planet had finally settled down following the destruction of the four planets. In the intervening centuries, a great many changes had occurred to the life that the planet generated. Gone were the experimental forms, all of the heavy and the weak. We would recognise most of the plants and animals that now inhabited the planet as many still exist today.

The transfer of mammals from Mars had been successful and early man had begun to divorce themselves away from the other primate groups. Most of the land was covered in trees and plants which sustained all of its huge diversity of life. Merlin walked the Earth and saw and wondered and enjoyed. He began to talk with and to work with all life. The planet rejoiced in all of its life and it too enjoyed. A golden time, a golden dawn.

The Faerie

The consciousness that is a star is capable of generating a great many forms of life. The planets that make up a star system are, usually, a part of the star's creation. The planets then go on to generate forms of life that are appropriate to themselves. Sometimes, within this generation process, the star will also generate life that is destined for particular planets.

With our solar system, things were a little different. Each of the planets are individual beings of an energy potential equivalent to that normally contained within a star. This means that our solar system has nine potential suns. This means that our nine planets encompass a considerable degree of potential for life creation. Add to this potential the fact that the higher life forms intended to live on these planets were also individual "souls", it meant that life could flourish as nowhere else within the universe.

However, the planet could not look after all of its life for itself and some of the responsibility normally has to be shared with the planet's other inhabitants. In the case of Earth, the responsibility was shared out between two groups. The animal life was to be, and still is, the responsibility of humans whilst the plant life is the responsibility of the Faerie.

The faerie are a part of the planet's generated life. In other words, as Earth's consciousness began to develop complex plants, as opposed to more simple organisms such as algae

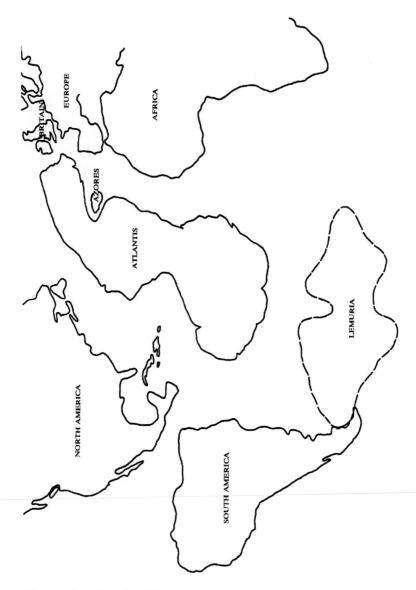

EUROPE

BRITAIN

AFRICA

AZORES

ATLANTIS

LEMURIA

NORTH AMERICA

SOUTH AMERICA

Illustration Number Two
Atlantis and Lemuria

40

which were generally seeded from other worlds, a form of life was required which could nourish and tend to the plants on the planet's behalf. To achieve this, the planet generated a collection of living, thinking beings whose primary purpose was to be Earth's "gardeners". So the faerie have been in existence as long as there has been life on this planet.

The realm of the faerie is vast and covers the whole world. All cultures have a name for the faerie and the etheric template which gives them life. In the west, we have come to know this template as Avalon.

Avalon exists in reality. It is the realm of the faerie, the "powerhouse" of energy that maintains all of their activities and gives them life. The world of the faerie encompasses a vast range of beings and entities from The Lady to the minute flower faerie.

It would be extremely unfair to suggest that a hierarchy exists within the faerie as each see their place within the whole and each have their extremely important role to play in the maintenance of our plant life. However, as with all things, there are those who contain larger quantities of energy potential than others and the same is true of the faerie.

At the "top" of this energy scale is The Lady. There is no other way to describe the one who is charged with the role of maintaining the land. Some call her The Queen but that is to imply rank and servitude and these are human traits and failings, not the faeries'.

The Lady is actually a soul who came to work with the Earth at the time the plant life was being formed. Her 'soul origin' is actually one of the six higher civilisations but has become so enmeshed within the energies of the planet that she has become one with the faerie. With the Lady are twenty six "Higher Guardians" and fifty two "Guardians", together with several thousand "managers", collectively known as the Sidhé (pronounced Shee). These supervise the work of many millions of faerie which fall into fifty two distinct groups.

We know the names of some of these but most are the secret of the faerie. The reason for this is that as man developed into the modern world, he began to abuse his position and privileges and the faerie moved into their "secret" realms to save themselves from human harm and these secret names were removed from our knowledge. The time is not yet right for man to regain this knowledge.

All of the faerie are workers with energy. They add, enhance and, above all, play with the energies of the Earth and the plants that are in their care. This is not to imply irresponsibility by the use of the word 'play' but is used to try to impart their sense of love, their sense of mischief, their sense of joy. The faerie love everything of this Earth and all of the life that it supports. They are incapable of anything other than this love and it is freely given with nothing expected in return.

Although their primary role is to work with and nurture the plant life of the planet, there are also those who work with the elements that make up the Earth's structure. The rocks and stones of the earth have an energy and there are faerie who work with these.

Flower faerie, gnomes, elves, dwarves, etc. are all names that the faerie are known by and these are based upon the names that they originally gave to themselves. Over the centuries, the original names have been corrupted down and altered to their current forms, the original forms of these words still belong to the faerie alone. But for now, our understanding of these names will suffice. These are human names, not faerie names. Their true names have a power to call them to you. Once we had this trust, this sharing of "power" in the times when Atlantis was still a fresh memory but, with the coming of organised religions that did not honour the Earth, the faerie withdrew and our close connection with them was lost to all but a few. This episode in human/faerie history will be discussed later.

When Merlin arrived on the planet, he and the Lady formed a bond which cannot be broken. It was and is a sharing of love and of purpose that transcends all else. Merlin cannot do other than to love the Earth and all of its life but with the Lady, their attachment extends beyond love, beyond life and beyond time. A partnership which will last as long as the Earth and beyond.

Human Development

Three and a half million years ago Merlin began his work with those who eventually became us. At the time, there were two distinct pre-human groups. There were those who had been originally developed by Earth, The Neanderthals, and there were the group, who were slightly more developed, brought from Mars when it became clear that life on that planet could no longer be sustained, Cro Magnon man.

There was no competition between these groups and Merlin began to work with both to evaluate their potential. Both groups had a "mass consciousness" which belonged to each group and each group had their own etheric template. Merlin worked within these regions of both groups to try to help both groups develop their own potential. Merlin was not there to judge the merits of a particular group, only to help both to progress as far and as rapidly as their potential would allow.

This work was carried out by sharing useful genetic characteristics and modifying the energy constructs around which these early humans were built. The nearest analogy to working in this way would be someone who works with clay to build models and statues. A basic framework is constructed, the etheric template, onto which is added layers of clay which form the finished piece. By altering or modifying each layer, the form of the finished piece can be gently and gradually altered. As the etheric template alters, so too does the mass consciousness and a group of individuals can be helped to develop in beneficial ways.

This work continued to a point where these early humans began to be aware of themselves, their world and their potential. At this point, Merlin stood back and allowed the early humans to develop at their own pace and in directions which they began to dictate. Freedom of choice underlies all within this universe and once a sufficient level of awareness was achieved, where they became aware that choice existed, they had to be allowed to develop by themselves and in their own ways.

The two groups began to change. One group developed quite rapidly and the other more slowly.

During this time, Merlin began to work in closer ways with The Lady to develop plants which could better sustain the developing early humans. New plant etheric templates were developed for types which produced seeds and fruits more suited to early human digestion. Many of these plants form the basis of our current diets. This was the real work of the faerie, to work with humanity, represented at this stage by Merlin, in developing the plants of the planet to sustain the future mankind.

The work with animals was a little different. The planet adopted or created but then developed the etheric templates for all of the animals on the planet. Some animals had been introduced from other worlds but these were "adopted" by the planet and the etheric templates of these animals became the Earth's. All of these animals were sustained and developed by the planet. However, as early man began to develop, he was made aware of the fact that he needed to play his role in sustaining planetary life.

Man's role was to work with the etheric templates of various animals and help to hold their presence on the planet. This was achieved by the tribal shaman working within the animals' mass consciousness, a kind of reinforcement of emotional bonds.

In this way, man began to lose his fear of animals and gradually domesticated several breeds. It was also in this way that several groups of animals were removed from the planet as they represented too large a threat to humanity's development. It is difficult to concentrate on developing spiritually and emotionally if you are constantly being distracted by an animal trying to make you its lunch.

Lemuria

Merlin continued to work with the early humans, or at least as far as they wanted him to and he continued his relationship with the faerie. The planned development of a fully aware being in a physical body was proceeding but at an extremely slow pace. Despite several modifications to the genetic structures and many changes within the mass consciousness, the anticipated rapid development was not forthcoming.

Merlin worked hard at trying to determine the root cause of this problem. Most of the life, in all of its many forms throughout the universe, had always progressed from its humbler beginnings into something more than just dense energy. The anticipated arrival of conscious man was considerably delayed. There had to be an answer but nobody, throughout the whole universe, could provide any clues.

Finally, Merlin invited the universe to come to Earth to help to resolve the problem. Those who came to study the problem were members of a civilisation which understood genetic structures and were the ones who had helped the Earth repopulate following the difficulties it had experienced with the loss of the four planets.

Merlin chose the best location for establishing their research facilities as an ice island off the coast of South America, a place we know as Lemuria. These visitors from NGC 584 were on Earth for approximately six thousand years and they arrived at what was eventually to prove only part of the answer.

The planetary consciousness had been unable to readjust fully from the earlier changes in the solar system. It had created a subtle wobble in the planet's magnetic flux and this was serving to alter the energy patterns within the planets' inhabitants. This was something which nobody had experienced before and it proved difficult to properly correct. Merlin was unaware that a problem of this nature could exist and the planetary consciousness could not diagnose the problem for itself. It was also a problem that had never existed on any other world. This new experiment was presenting a greater range of problems than anyone had anticipated.

Once the problem was diagnosed, work was begun to rectify it. Merlin, as representative of The Thirteen, joined with the six higher civilisations, the seven lower civilisations and the planet to correct the problem and bring about a position where the experiment could continue.

Merlin's role was to construct a new energy matrix. This was a grid work of energy lines which criss-crossed the whole globe, this is what we now call the Lay Line grid. This helped to stabilise the planet's energies and provided a new source of energy for the planet from the universal limitless supply. The main "interchange" for these energies was at Silbury Hill in Wiltshire, where it remained as the most powerful energy intake point on the planet until the new grid was connected in August 1996. Silbury was chosen because it was a key point in the planet's own energy structures. It was here that the 'wobble' was focussed. By adding energy into this point, the flux variations could most easily be corrected and balanced. The greatest point of concentration of the planet's own energy fields is still located at West Kennet Long Barrow which is directly opposite Silbury Hill.

Once the correction work was complete, the Earth was left to itself for nine thousand years. Merlin did not leave the planet during this time but worked with the planet and tried to rectify some of the problems encountered by the early humans during the problem period.

To a certain extent, he succeeded and the Earth and its inhabitants were ready for the next phase.

As a result of the problems caused by the removal of the four planets, a great deal of time had been lost and a plan was put forward, by Merlin, to accelerate the development of humanity.

The plan was agreed by all of those involved with the Earth and eighty five thousand years ago, Atlantis was established.

Chapter Three

Atlantis

Atlantis was a continent between North America and Europe. It was chosen because its Northern shores were close to the Silbury Hill energy intake, it had a climate which represented the average of the weather patterns on the globe and it contained only a limited number of pre-human primates. It was also isolated from all other land masses. In legend, it became known as the Garden of Eden.

The continent began at Britain, wrapped around the Azores and ended in what is now the Caribbean basin. The South American continent was not in its current position but located further out into the Pacific Ocean (see illustration number two).

Along its back were a central chain of mountains which sent off little spurs of mountains along the way. The height of the mountains varied from low hills to permanently snow capped peaks. Around the hills and mountains flowed many rivers which were clear and sparkling and contained many varieties of fish and other creatures.

Between the mountains were broad regions of forest broken by sweeping grassy plains dotted with numerous fresh water lakes. Around the coastline were many cliffs and many sandy beaches. In the North were broadleaf woodlands whilst in the South were tropical palms. Many animals roamed the land and there were isolated pockets of pre-human primates.

Amongst the central mountains was a chain of active volcanoes which occasionally erupted with violence spreading ash and lava for many miles around the peaks. It was not a peaceful land but nor was it dangerous. Those who lived there knew its ways and lived in harmony with the land.

There were no settlements as such, just small groups of pre-humans living in a variety of shelters and caves. They knew their land and how to obtain the best from it. They were not 'savages', just a part of their natural world.

All of the pre-human primates, over the whole planet, were consulted before Atlantis was established. The primates had developed to a point where they could understand a little of who they were and the implications of the work proposed to be carried out on Atlantis. Freedom of choice was paramount.
If all of these primates had decided that they did not wish to be a part of the proposed work, Atlantis would never have been established. However, a number were intrigued by the possibilities on offer and readily agreed to take part. Those who were on Atlantis, and did not want to take part, were moved to another region of the planet, of their own choosing and helped, as they requested, to establish themselves in their new environment.

The first to arrive were a group of beings from NGC 584. During their time on Lemuria, they concentrated on the work on the planet itself and had spent very little time working with the pre-human primates. They had only observed the activities and level of development and had not worked on them directly. Their purpose now was to study the pre-humans and develop ways in which their progress could be accelerated.

Their landing took place on a grassy plain in the south of the continent and this is where the first settlement was established. The craft they arrived in were used as living and laboratory space for a long time before any structures were built on the land.

At this stage in human development, our energy structures were not fully developed. The seven physical chakras were in place but they were not fully formed and as they were, essentially, more part of the planetary consciousness than fully aware individuals, they did not have the six higher chakras that make up the connection to the higher self.

Development took place from two directions.

The first was to alter their genetic structures so that the body form became more like ours. This was achieved by the introduction of DNA sequences we know as accelerator genes. This was genetic engineering in its purest form.
There was a situation where, by no fault of their own, these primates had been held back in their development. It had only recently been discovered that the problem lay with the disruption to the Earth's rotation and energy structures brought about by the explosion of the two planets and steps needed to be taken where the lack of progress could be made good. These genetic modifications were designed to do just that, to bring these pre humans to the point they should have been had the problems not occurred.

The method employed to introduce these genes was also non intrusive and non harmful. An energy construction was made which carried a programme sequence which was designed to work with the individual the programme was attached to. These programmers were constructed of pure energy and they were introduced into the body without any harm being done to the individual concerned. These 'programmers' were constructed a little like a cut diamond. They had six facets with a flat top with the facets coming to a single point. with each facet carrying an aspect of the programme (see illustration number three).

Once installed, the programmer "read" the DNA of the participant and slowly made adjustments to the primary gene sequences. These adjustments were made whilst the individual was fully conscious and did not disrupt their life in any way. Very subtle adjustments were made in this way and the body form began to change. As these individuals reproduced, the corrected gene sequences were passed on to their offspring and the work accelerated. Within three generations, the pre-human primates had changed from their crude, primate like bodies to the body form we currently have. At the same time as these genetic changes were occurring, Merlin was altering the etheric template of these primates to reflect the changing body form. From this point onwards, humans and primates would forever be separated.

Human Mass Consciousness

The primates are part of the planet's being with an etheric template and mass consciousness, a group soul, which is sustained by the joint efforts of the planet and humanity. Although the pre-human primates had been a part of this group soul at the beginning, as they developed, they generated their own mass consciousness. By creating a new, specific etheric template, Merlin effectively created a new species with their own mass consciousness which increasingly became divorced from the planetary consciousness. Although this was a necessary part of human development, as we have reduced in awareness we have taken this to mean that we are detached from the planet and its life and given us our arrogance and sense of being above all planetary life.

Whilst the refinements to the mass consciousness and etheric template were taking place, other developments were happening which also helped with the whole advancement process.

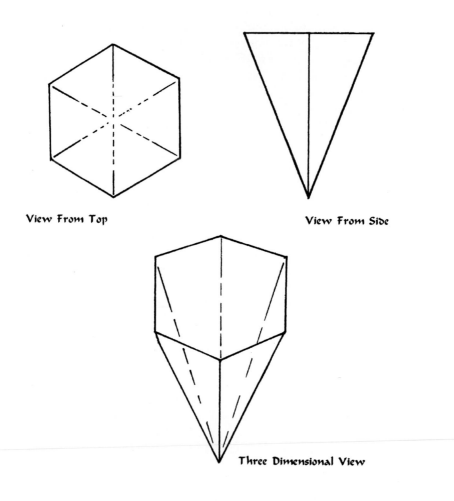

View From Top   View From Side

Three Dimensional View

Illustration Number Three
An Atlantean Energy DNA 'Programmer'

These developments should be seen for what they were. We currently have a very jaundiced view of genetic engineering and most people fear the work the scientists are currently undertaking. These fears are justified as the current experiments begin to unlock many peoples' memories of the end of Atlantis where bizarre experimentation put many souls into torment and ultimately resulted in the destruction of the continent. Current genetic experimentation has the potential to bring about the same kind of destruction but this time it would happen on a global scale.

These early genetic modifications, primarily with Cro Magnon Man, were carried out with a specific purpose in mind and that purpose was carried out with a purity of intent that we cannot now fully understand. If you have no ulterior motive, such as material profit, then all of your actions come from the heart and it was from this viewpoint that these actions and modifications were carried out. If the soul is pure, there can be nothing but purity of thought and action - a position very rarely encountered on Earth in the past few thousand years.

Another line of approach was to blend together 'human' genes and the genes of the species most closely resembling humans, the Pleiadeans.

The sperm of a Cro Magnon was mixed with the egg of a Pleiadean female and the birth of a new species took place. All beings have a soul, the soul of this new first born was that of Merlin. As representative of the thirteen on Earth, one of Merlin's roles is to be the first to experience all which humanity was likely to experience. Up until this stage, Merlin had maintained an only partial physical form. This new birth process allowed him to experience the pre-human physical body for the first time. By using this process, it was possible to experience full physical being for the first time and many invaluable lessons were learned about the nature of physical life.

Up until this point, Merlin had existed between the two worlds. The world of 'angelic' energy and the world of physical density. This middle route had allowed him to work with the planet's consciousness, the faerie and the primates with equal ease, this change gave him the opportunity to assist the rapidly developing primates in much more direct and practical ways.

Very few were born in this way, at this stage, as the intention was to develop the primates to a point where full conscious awareness was possible. This form of hybrid took away from that process by mixing other genetic material into the human gene pool. The genetic acceleration work carried out by those from NGC 584 worked only with the Cro Magnon genetic structures and smoothed out the rough edges.

With the physical and genetic work completed, the next phase was to begin to introduce increasing levels of consciousness. In energy terms, these new humans had all seven physical chakras intact and functioning, the six higher chakras were formed in outline but had no substance, no energy components with which to complete their development. At this point, Merlin fulfilled one of his other roles, that of a creationary force, and introduced this missing energy. As this conscious energy was introduced, the physical body began to undertake further changes and began to change in density. The dense physical bodies began to become lighter and less dense. A process began which formed a loop. The more the body lightened, the more consciousness they could absorb, the more consciousness they absorbed, the less dense the body became. In this sense, a full, conscious, aware human has seven fully integrated chakras (total consciousness), thirteen strands to their DNA spirals and a physical body which has less density than ours. Only 1358 were created in this way and means that these souls are the only true Earth humans. These "first born" of the Earth are the conscious beings which, eventually, formed the basis for all future human etheric templates and are, essentially, the indigenous, aboriginal peoples of the world.

At last, the goal was achieved. A fully aware, fully conscious, physical being stood on the Earth. Humanity was born.

Paraδíse

It is difficult to describe the sense of achievement felt by all of those concerned. Here, the seemingly impossible had been achieved and Merlin's role had been fulfilled. It was time to relax and enjoy the paradise of Earth.

These new First Born humans were very special. They were considerably in advance of our capabilities and understanding. Only now, as we begin our final climb back to full awareness, can we even begin to glimpse some of the reality of consciousness integration.

Try to imagine standing in a glade of trees and being able to see the energies of each tree, each blade of grass, each droplet of water and to be able to communicate and interact with each of these energies. To stand with the faerie and join in their games of joy. To communicate with fellow humans, individually and en mass, by thought alone. To communicate with those of other worlds and realms, to be a part of the angels. To be able to travel freely around Atlantis, or even the planet by thought alone. Think of where you want to be and carry the body along with the thought. To see the joy in its life that a flower has. A time of wonder and of fulfilment. A true paradise gained. This is how life continued for the next nine thousand years.

Many of those from the other universal races came to visit and some stayed to enjoy what had been created. Although shelter was not required for any of Atlantis' inhabitants, forms of art developed which resulted, amongst many other avenues, in architecture and permanent buildings were built for the first time on the surface of the Earth. These buildings were amazing structures which wove together the fabric of the earth and the energy of the stars, buildings breathtaking in their complexity and beauty. All forms of artistic pursuits were undertaken which enhanced our understanding of what life is capable of achieving. Even the animals joined into these joyous undertakings. If you can communicate directly with all animals and have no need to hunt, even wild animals will relax and become part of our everyday world.

There was no crime, no fear, no want, all coexisted peacefully and harmoniously.

During this time, Merlin was busy building new energies to meet the growing demand. The energy matrix grid was extended and enhanced to provide greater complexities and frequencies of energy to allow for greater possibility and creativity. Huge crystal energy sources were built to enhance this flow and provide very specific frequencies for specific tasks. Many of these crystals were built on the islands of the Azores which became a secondary power house of energy to feed the many demands. The energies of these crystals were very different from those obtained through Silbury Hill. Silbury is an intake point from off the planet whilst these crystals were built of the earth and could be tuned to very specific frequencies.

Genetic Manipulation

As our relationships with the animals developed, some individuals became interested in altering their appearance to take on some of the characteristics of their favourite animals. This involved using the 'diamond' shaped energy crystals used to accelerate Cro Magnon man to bring about genetic manipulations to change, for example, skin colour or texture to mimic the skin patterns of a chosen animal.

Many took on leopard skins, tiger skins, snake skins, etc. which were not worn as coats but their own skin was altered to be of these patterns and textures. It was a recognition of our responsibility towards the animal world, a blending of those who worked with the mass consciousness of particular animal groups and their "totem" animals. These initial changes of skin were carried out as a mark of respect, an acknowledgement of the beauty of the animal concerned. Eventually, some saw it as a fashion and began to adopt animal characteristics as a means of expression and, as these kinds of genetic manipulation techniques became easier, some would even change these patterns to suit their whims. This was the beginning of a slippery slope downwards.

A slow and subtle change had been occurring during the past millennia which had not been noticed, the reasons for this change were not resolved until some time after the end of Atlantis, but was eventually noticed as a slowing down of the energy frequencies of many of the inhabitants. This change was very gradual and the consequences of this change created many problems.

The biggest was the way in which these experiments with the characteristics of animals became increasingly bizarre. It began with trying to mix the characteristics of one animal with another. These were largely unsuccessful as the etheric templates could not accommodate this level of change. Some attempted to develop new templates and some succeeded. The next level of change was to mix animal traits with those of humans. These were far more successful.

A human life time, at this stage, spanned an average of over one thousand years. The difference between the soul being in the body and the soul leaving the body, in energy awareness terms, was not that great and it was possible to design genetic matrices which could alter body shapes, or parts of the body. If you designed one of these matrices when you were alive, it was possible to adopt the new genetic structures into a subsequent new body when you returned. In this way, it was possible to grow a human head on an animal's body or an animal head on a human body whilst maintaining the integrity of the human soul. Freedom of choice allows for all possibilities to be explored. The human etheric template was not affected as these experiments were undertaken by individuals who could alter their own energetic structures to accommodate such a level of change. It was accepted by others as freedom of choice and freedom of expression could not be taken away.

Within certain sections of the community, genetic material began to become very mixed. This level of mixing led to some animal character traits becoming a part of these people's own make up and human predators began to appear.

If you mix together the cunning and single mindedness of a wild cat and an enquiring mind, the results lead to the aggressive taking of people for experimental purposes. This is why some people's memories of Atlantis are of pain and suffering. These are people who managed to survive these experiments, but there were also many souls who became so tortured by these experiments that they felt unable to continue in their existence.

Finally, most of these abductions and experiments were stopped by the concerted will of the people pointing out the error of the ways of these experimenters and they were banished from the planet to begin a period of rehabilitation amongst the six higher civilisations. Freedom of choice cannot be taken away, but when one individual's freedom to choose takes away another's freedom to choose it cannot be tolerated. This illustrates the dangers of mixing genetic material from different species. Even with our almost full conscious awareness at this time, mistakes were made and some people found a way of removing the free choice of others when the predatory aspects of an animal's genetic makeup were accidentally transferred into the human with the results proving to be totally unpredictable and ultimately, disastrous.

The Destruction of Atlantis

Earth was abundant with life of all varieties. It is so successful that it contains a greater number of forms of life than the rest of the universe put together. Many of the species were, with minor genetic and energetic modifications, suitable for other worlds. Many species were copied in this way and given new life on and to other worlds. One of these modified life forms went wrong.

The simplest, but usually most useful forms of life on most planets is bacteria. There are many thousands of forms on Earth, all of which are beneficial (they only become harmful when they multiply beyond their normal levels). One strain of bacteria developed on Earth was intended to have enormous benefits on another, newly developing world. This bacteria had been designed to have the capability of converting oxygen to hydrogen. As hydrogen was the primary gas on this other planet, this bacteria would prove useful as it could also be modified to alter other substances and other gasses to hydrogen.

Somehow, this bacteria entered into the food supply and was ingested by a number of people. The bacteria was slow acting and remained undetected for a long time before the consequences were fully realised. The bacteria also had the capability of modifying itself in the same way as most bacteria do, and it was only properly noticed when one of its modifications became airborne. This bacteria was changing the atmosphere and the water into hydrogen. The implication was that if this bacteria spread away from Atlantis, it would destroy all life on Earth.

A collective decision was made to contain this bacteria. This could only be achieved by the complete destruction of Atlantis and all of the life that carried this bacteria with them.

A perimeter trench was opened around the whole continent, deep enough to reach the planet's magma core. The resulting ring of volcanoes created an atmosphere which killed off all of the airborne bacteria. The volcanoes then collapsed in on themselves, totally enveloping the continent and taking it into the Earth's core.

Chapter Four

After Atlantis

Almost everything was lost.

A huge rescue operation had been undertaken before the final destruction was enacted. All animals were inspected for bacterial infection and all of those uninfected had been removed to the continents either side of the Atlantic (Noah's Ark). The human or non terrestrial life that had not been infected left the continent and went to other lands (one who left, but carried the bacteria, gave rise to the biblical story of Lot's wife who was turned into 'a pillar of salt'. If you convert all of the oxygen in the body to hydrogen, the result is the body's tissues turn to a mineral substance not unlike salt). All those who had been infected gave up their lives with the continent. Sodom and Gomorra had been destroyed and its sinking generated the flood.

Opening up the floor of the Atlantic ocean in this way created a fault line that sunk the Mediterranean, forming a sea. It also altered the fault lines in the Pacific basin and South America moved to its current location. Many regions around the world were affected by shock wave movements. Seventy thousand years ago, the face of the planet changed. Everything moved into a state of flux. Those who had escaped moved to lands they chose. Many moved to Britain and Ireland, the West African coast was colonised, most of those who carried the results of their genetic experiments moved to Egypt and a few to South America.

The Egyptian ones became a part of legends and god like figures as they still retained some of their higher brain functions. In South America, one figure, above all, became the basis of much that was to follow on that continent. This was an androgynous figure whose skin was that of a diamond backed rattlesnake and whose head was covered in long blond hair. A plumed serpent who became known as Quetzalcoatl.

Merlin also eventually moved to South America. He and the Lady went to live on the slopes of Machu Pichu. They needed some time to reflect on events and to formulate a plan for humanity.

Where to go? What to do? Should the plan for humanity be abandoned? If it was to restart, where and how? Would the planet wish to continue?

In energy terms, the lay line grid had been saved by detaching Atlantis from Silbury Hill just before the continent was sunk. The Azores energy source had been lost with Atlantis as there was a danger that the bacteria was present there. At least the planet's energies were intact even if they were a little shaken. To help reinforce and repair the lay line grid, a new, temporary intake point was created by Merlin at Machu Pichu. Although no longer active, the mountain still retains its air of energetic importance from this time.

Following a long period of thought and consideration of all of the options, Merlin decided to allow the Earth to fully recover and the pre-humans to develop by themselves.

The fate of those who had been on Atlantis at its end fell into several groups.

Those who had been most tortured by their experiments into animal forms died with the continent, including their souls - something never before seen and the whole universe mourned their loss. Those who were physical and contaminated by the bacteria, about 60% of the population, left their physical bodies and returned to their home worlds many of whom vowing never to take on human form again. These included all of the universal races.

Those who remained on the planet began to establish settlements where they had "landed" after the destruction. This group, about 150 000 people, set up shelters and began to learn about their locality. These locations included Southern Britain, the West African coast, parts of the Mediterranean coast line, Mesopotamia, the Pacific Islands and South America.

Most were in a state of shock at the magnitude of the destruction and many lived out their life spans and then returned to their home world. Those who remained mainly took to travelling around the planet. Occasionally they encountered groups of pre-humans but these encounters were kept to a minimum. Never the less, these encounters did begin to establish legends which lodged in the mass consciousness which later formed the basis for a number of religious beliefs.

Eventually, all of the Atlanteans died out, a gradual process that took about 1500 years.

Earth was left to its own devices. Merlin and the Lady rested and enjoyed the world as it was. They stayed mainly at Machu Pichu but travelled the planet mending, repairing, modifying and occasionally creating a new species of plant to suit specific locations.

Eventually, the energies were repaired and the planet was finally at peace.

Adult Birth

But, Merlin could not rest there. He had been charged with a task by the Thirteen and the task still needed to be fulfilled. Although the goal had been achieved on Atlantis, it had also been lost. A new form of approach needed to be formulated which could bring about the ultimate goal.

Many of the members of the six had enjoyed their time on Earth and those who had been created on Earth, the First Born, also wished to return. Many visits were made by these individuals to Merlin during this time and they were keeping a close eye on the developments taking place with the pre-human groups.

These groups had been developing, but very slowly, and would not be in a suitable position for "full" integration for very many thousands of years. Although they could reason and work with tools, they could not accommodate a higher level of consciousness. This was because their physical and energetic structures were extremely slow to develop.

Finally, a new form of approach was decided upon and twenty eight thousand years ago, Merlin and a group who represented the six higher civilisations, visited all of the pre-human groups on the planet. The purpose of the visit was to ask permission to establish several regions of the planet where a number of the six, which included the 'First Born' of Earth, could try a new form of "birth" process.

The pre-humans fully understood what was being asked of them and all agreed. Regions were located and the preparation work was begun.

Twenty eight thousand years ago a new energy grid was begun. Although the old grid, laid down in the days before Atlantis, still existed, it required modification for this new phase of development. With the destruction of Atlantis, the grid matrix had been severely disrupted and emergency measures had been taken to cut Atlantis off from the rest of the world. Silbury hill was, and still is, functional, but a new, more powerful matrix needed to be constructed. This new matrix needed to be flexible in order to accommodate potential future change. It also needed to be expanded so that it could accommodate the existing life on the planet and supply all of the energy needs for the incoming new.

Thirteen new energy centres were constructed. Twelve major centres and a new, more powerful intake centre. The twelve were located around the globe with the new intake located in north Somerset in Britain. Britain was, and still is, the main energy interchange on the planet. Silbury Hill was still useful but a new intake was required which could accommodate far higher ranges of energy frequencies. Silbury Hill is "locked" into the planet's energies and interchanges with West Kennet but this new energy intake needed to be freely available to anyone who had the need for its new frequency ranges.

Everything settled into place and, twenty thousand years ago, the first of the new arrivals came to Earth. These were mainly people who had been on Atlantis, a mix of The Six, Pleiadeans and NGC 584, and wanted to try to understand and resolve the problems encountered then.

They arrived as a pure energy form and adopted the etheric template formed with the first born in Atlantis. This template had temporarily become part of the planet's energy structures and it released the template to the arriving new humans.

By adopting the template in this fashion, the new humans became rapidly integrated into the life of the planet and took on energy patterns which coincided with the Earth's. The adoption of these energy frequencies were later to cause many problems but our current patterns of energy frequency were formed by these first arrivals. Once they had taken on the energy form, they began to use the physical elements of the planet to give themselves physical density and structure. Literally building their bodies out of the mud of the Earth (the origin of the Adam and Eve story although the story has been twisted to suggest that man came first and then woman. At this stage in our history, the arrivals were androgynous and the division into the sexes did not occur until much later. It was only when the decision to adopt sexual reproduction was taken that men became men and women became women). Six regions were chosen for this new beginning: South America; Mesopotamia; Egypt and Ethiopia; a region that included parts of Britain, Ireland and Northern France; Tibet and Southern Greece. The regions are listed in what was considered their order of importance.

The numbers of these new arrivals was quite small, overall there were only two thousand one hundred and fifty. These were the vanguard of a potentially new form of humanity and it was deemed prudent to limit their numbers until the implications of this new life were understood.

The destruction of Atlantis had been necessary because of the potential loss of all life on the planet but it had been noticed that changes had occurred within the energy structures of many individuals which were reducing their available energies. This amounted to a drop in consciousness potential and it was very worrying especially as nobody knew the reason why.

Once again the goal had been achieved - fully conscious physical beings walked on the surface of the Earth.

During this time, the primate humans were left to their own devices. This does not mean that they were abandoned, but were left to develop by themselves and in their own ways. The agreement was that these new arrivals lived in their own regions, or interacted with each other across the continents but even then, only within the regions of those visited. The new humans also monitored their progress from a distance and attempted to find ways in which the primate humans could be helped. Assistance would only be provided to those who asked for it, freedom of choice was paramount, but it would be useful to know what types of help could be provided if the request was made.

Chapter Five

Human Development

The removal of the continent of Atlantis had many far reaching repercussions as far as the planet was concerned. The global weather and climate at the time of Atlantis, and before, was very different to what it is today. At the time of its coming into being, the Earth's axis was vertical. This meant that the variation between seasons were negligible and the North Pole was not frozen. The whole of the planet's surface enjoyed a warm climate with little in the way of extremes of weather, the only frozen area was the South Pole. The problems caused by the removal of the four planets had established a 'wobble' in the Earth's rotation which generated major problems with the planet's weather patterns as well as annihilating the majority of life. It took several millennia for the planet to return to a more normal pattern of weather and prevent the periodic freezing of the planet's surface. Since the last freezing (Ice Age) ended one million years ago, the planet had settled into a return of its previous patterns of weather but with greater seasonal variations.

The destruction of Atlantis had taken this 'wobble' beyond the limits where the planet could hold its stability and it slipped into a new axis angle, the one we have today. The affects of the axis shift, combined with the sinking of a continent, were extremely far reaching.

Prior to the sinking of Atlantis, the continents had been in a 'settled' position. The surface of the continents were comparatively flat to that of today and there was very little in the way of volcanic activity. With the sinking of the continent, the whole of the planet's crust had to settle into new positions and this set up huge movements. For example, all of the crust's expansion points moved to new positions, South America moved to its present location, several large islands around Australia sank, Africa's Rift Valley opened and India moved northwards creating the Himalayas and altered the Tibetan plains. The Mediterranean Sea was formed, the Black Sea was flooded and the Alps were formed from a range of low hills. The North Pole had changed from being a temperate region to being frozen over.

It took ten thousand years for the Earth to settle and it was only then that life could be assessed anew.

Sixty thousand years ago, Merlin and the Lady began to repair the damage. The climate had now changed radically and new plants were needed to be created and the etheric template of many animals needed to be altered to accommodate the changes of climate. Most of the world's animals were used to conditions where the climate was warm and hospitable, with the advent of a true winter season and the accompanying shortage of food, many animals needed to adopt a period of hibernation. This could only be achieved by an alteration of their etheric template and this was the work undertaken by Merlin. The same work on plants was carried out by the Lady and the Sidhé.

The planet's life underwent a radical change and most of the behaviour patterns of both plants and animals that we see today had their beginnings at this time.

With new life forms developed and many of the existing forms modified to suit the new climate, the planet and all of its life were allowed to rest and to develop in their own ways (evolve).

When everything had stabilised, Merlin and the Lady reassessed the situation.

The world was very different. All life had changed in one way or another. There were new climatic conditions, new topography and new regions to be explored and populated. Plant and animal life had changed and were finding new ways of living within their new world.

The pre humans were also adapting and changing to the new world around them. The changed planet helped them to grow and develop as the new challenges of life presented obstacles to be overcome and this enhanced their mental and reasoning skills.

Beginning Again
What to do?

Should the Earth be left to its own devices? Should life be allowed to find its own way to evolve to accommodate the new? Could or even should a new Atlantis be established? Would the pre human groups now develop more rapidly with their greater challenges in life?

The concept behind Earth was the desire to form a high density, fully conscious being. It had been proven possible by the success of Atlantis. With only some of the problems that had necessitated the destruction of Atlantis understood, it was felt best to allow life to take its natural course and see if it was possible for the planet's pre humans to develop by themselves. This is how life continued and developed for the next forty thousand years.

Merlin and the Lady watched and waited.

The idea of forty thousand years as a period of watching and waiting is almost beyond our comprehension. It should be remembered that both Merlin and the Lady were in a non physical state, an energy form. In this form time takes on a different scale. We are accustomed to one second following another in a linear fashion building each minute and each year. In a condition of pure energy, the consciousness does not register time in this way. At higher frequencies of being, time has its own energy and the frequencies of this energy do not register the seconds as they pass. Rather, there is a spiral of energies which can transport the consciousness to any point within its vortex. In this way, the forty thousand year time span to us was nothing more than a swirl of energy to Merlin and the Lady.

This does not mean that they were idle during this period. An understanding of the conditions which had led to the mayhem and destruction of Atlantis still needed to be understood and a solution found. Without this knowledge, the experiment of Earth would fail.

Everything within this universe is comprised of energy and, therefore, the problem with higher life on Earth must have an energetic cause and an energetic answer. In order to study the problem, Merlin asked that several members of the Six Higher Civilisations, who had lived in Atlantis, to return to Earth and take on human form. This was achieved by making use of the human etheric template and condensing energies to form the organs etc. In other words, an adult without birth and childhood.

By studying these humans over a period of time, it was possible to understand why Atlantis had gone so badly wrong. In order to exist at a truly physical density, the planet had established a base energy frequency of 7.56 Hz (cycles per second). This frequency underlies all life on the planet and is the base frequency of the root chakra for all life. In order to remain on the planet, these higher beings needed to adopt this frequency otherwise they remained in the pure energy form of the Six. The higher frequencies of the higher elements of the consciousness can run up to several hundreds of thousands cycles per second and the adoption of the 7.56 Hz base note began to draw the energies of the consciousness into the physical form reducing the energy components available to the soul when made physical. Over a period of time, the higher energies became depleted and the physical form increased in density, reducing the capabilities of the higher brain functions. This also explained why the pre human primates were very slow in developing their potential. As fully physical beings, it would be extremely difficult to overcome the planet's energies and reach full consciousness awareness. With the underlying problem identified, it was now a question of finding a solution.

At this stage in human development there were two basic groups on the planet. Neanderthal man had been a product of evolution of the primates created by the planet and Cro Magnon man had been introduced from Mars when that planet had lost all of its life by the destruction of the two planets. It was to these two groups that Merlin now turned.

Given the problems encountered with the planet's own energies and the base note frequencies, the solution seemed to lay in accelerating the development of the two human groups. Both groups were approached and fully appraised of the proposal. Nothing could begin unless one or both agreed to the proposals - free choice is paramount.

The Neanderthals generally decided to develop on their own. They were a part of the planet's creation and wished to take whatever course the planet took. This was entirely their decision. As other developments progressed their numbers gradually declined until all that remains now of their numbers are an isolated pocket on the Russian and Chinese border (several eyewitness accounts by border guards attest to this).

Cro Magnon's story is a little different.

The current genetic archaeological evidence is that there is no link whatsoever between humanity (homo sapien sapien) and Neanderthal and for once the scientists are on the right track. The Neanderthal story is maintained within the Akashic but for all intents and purposes they have not played any role in the development of the human race. This really appears to be neither good nor bad, just the exercising of choices and their resulting consequences. The planet makes no comments beyond this record and sees their demise in the same way as the others of its creations which disappeared before Atlantis. However, the destruction of animal species since humanity took over all aspects of planetary life is a very different story and one which the planet takes a very different view.

A Fresh Start

The work with Cro Magnon man now began with the development of higher energy etheric templates. The energy patterns of the First Born of Atlantis were to be utilised eventually but intermediate stages needed to be progressed and this was Merlin's first task.

In order to assist in Merlin's work, he had asked members of the six non physical civilisations and some of the NGC and Pleiadean to live on Earth and adopt a physical form. This allowed them to carry out some investigation work into the problems previously encountered on Atlantis.

Six areas of the Earth were visited by these groups and small 'colonies' established. The areas established were in Britain, France, Tibet, China, Sumeria and Africa.

Once the work with the Cro Magnon was begun, the new arrivals from other worlds were approached and they began to assist and interact with those of the early humans who had decided to work with this change.

The six groups had been exploring and experiencing. Life was a new adventure and all was there to begin anew. Most of the sorrier lessons of Atlantis had been learned and these new humans had been very cautious about their interactions and actions.

Merlin spent an amount of his time travelling between each group checking on their actions and energies. He also continued to work with the Sidhé and slowly introduced each new human group to the faerie and the ways of the Sidhé.

All began to flourish and the new humans and the Sidhé forged a deep relationship which was not broken for many thousands of years. Incidentally, Merlin is a name given by the Sidhé. The closest translation would be 'The Creator of Energies'.

Following about two hundred years of this level of existence, these new humans decided to adopt a gender. Androgyny was fine but sex looked interesting and sexual reproduction began. The population began to slowly rise and the process allowed for others, of the six higher civilisations, to experience human birth for themselves.

Sex at this level of being is much more than how we experience it. The link is just not between two physical bodies but between two souls. This is a totally shared experience that lifts the limitations of the human body into the realms of the higher self. This is a total exchange of being and one which we are gradually returning towards as our current changes progress.

The Cro Magnon form developed rapidly and their body form was modified by accelerator genetic sequences, similar to the Atlantean accelerators. Within three generations, the combination of accelerators and modifications to the etheric template produced homo sapien sapien. There is no missing link, just an acceleration of natural evolution from one form to another.

With the six groups from the six higher civilisations adopting sexual reproduction and the developing humans becoming closer to each other in both energetic and physical terms, many from the six groups began to be born to the human groups as a means of determining how to progress.

Gradually, this process took over and, over a period of centuries, the only inhabitants on Earth, in a human form, were those of the six higher civilisations and the planet's First Born. Once again, Merlin's goal had been achieved - a fully physical, fully conscious being was on Earth.

Now began the process of finding out how to overcome the problem of the Earth's energies slowing down the higher consciousness functions.

Sidhe Development
Along with this change came others. The Sidhé had been watching these developments quite closely and began to look at the possibility of their experiencing a physical existence for themselves.

There were two processes by which this could be achieved. The first was to modify the Sidhé's own energetic makeup in order for them to match the human etheric template and therefore to be born in the human way. To this end the planet worked with Merlin to bring about this level of change for those of the Sidhé who chose to do so. Whilst it had a novelty value, very few of the Sidhé took this route and the idea was abandoned after one lifetime.

The second way was to build what came to be known as a 'Starchamber'. This was an energy construction a little like a cave and lined with crystals of a similar construction to those used in Atlantis. This cave provided a huge amount of energy which could be 'tuned' to provide all of the frequencies necessary to transfer from the Sidhé's pure energy form and condense it into the physical on a temporary basis. This proved to be much more popular as you walked into the chamber as a Sidhé in energy form and walked out as a Sidhé in physical form, capable of acting and interacting on a fully physical level.

This chamber was also used to blend together the soul of a Sidhé and the soul of one of the six higher civilisations - a Sidhé/human hybrid. This was achieved once or twice with each of the civilisations active on Earth but never attempted again as the merging became permanent.

The Sidhé are of this Earth and as such cannot travel to other worlds. This is because they are made of the energy of the Earth and can only exist whilst attached to the planet's consciousness. The arrival of the six groups meant that the Sidhé became curious about other worlds and how life there existed. They expressed a desire to travel to other worlds in order to learn of their life and to see if any could be adopted for Earth.

Their energy structures meant that they could not travel beyond the energy of the Earth and so they adopted a physical form to see if this could overcome their limitations. However, this modification to their form proved only to be a limited success in this respect and only allowed travel around the solar system. Despite taking on a physical form, their basic energy makeup did not allow them to travel beyond the solar system's energy envelope.

To overcome these difficulties and to satisfy their curiosity about other worlds, some Pleiadeans volunteered to give those of the Sidhé who wished for the experience, an energy 'piggy back'. In order to do this, the member of the Sidhé and the Pleiadeans entered the 'star chamber' and consciously merged their energies. The intention was that once they returned from their journeys, the process would be reversed and the two merged beings could return to their original identities. Unfortunately, the process proved to be irreversible and that was why so few of these merges were carried out.

Human Completion

By about eighteen thousand years ago the human population was entirely composed of the modified Cro Magnon form with the consciousness, the soul of each individual originating from members of the six higher civilisations.

Prior to achieving the new human physical structures, each person had been an individual but did not have what could be described as an individual soul. Both the Neanderthal and Cro Magnon pre human forms had their etheric templates maintained by the planet. In the same way as animals, each individual was connected to a 'group soul', an integrated mass consciousness. By the soul now arriving from the realms of the 'Angels', the six higher civilisations, a new mass consciousness was formed where each individual played a part and was connected but was also a complete individual. This ultimately took the human etheric template and mass consciousness away from the planet's direct control and humanity became a form of life independent of the planetary consciousness but still living within its influence.

These events take us to about fifteen thousand years ago. At this time, the planet had settled into its new rhythms of weather following the trauma of the sinking of Atlantis. Plants and animals were more or less as they are now and humanity was in its final, current, form. There were winters of quite severe cold but there were no major icings over of the planet's surface. The six groups had expanded and the population was beginning to grow as many of the six higher civilisations came to experience physical life. There were also occasional visitors from the seven lower civilisations particularly from the Pleiadeans and NGC 584.

Life was harmonious and each group travelled freely about the planet and interacted with each other. Travel was not undertaken by the use of any craft. One of the higher brain functions we have lost is the ability to think yourself somewhere and then carry the body along the thought, true translocation. Bi location was also possible where an individual could literally be in two places at once - only partial body relocation. We could interact and communicate with all animals and plants. The beginnings of herbalism arose at this time, it was a question of 'asking' a plant what its properties were and how those properties could interact with the human body. This is ultimately how all plants received their natural names.

Slowly, very slowly, changes began to occur.

The planet's base note frequency, 7.56 Hz, was acting as anticipated and slowly condensing the higher frequency levels of the higher elements of the consciousness.

Merlin began to develop energetic means of overcoming these problems. The starchamber could be modified to enhance the higher level energies to bring them back to full function but proved to be only a temporary respite.

Energy points were built on the Earth's surface at Stonehenge, the Sphinx, Teotehuacan, Machu Pichu etc. which were aligned through the Orion Gate to bring in clean, pure energy from deep within the galaxy. All proved to be only

78

fully effective whilst the individual was standing within the energy stream.

Others began to work on potential physical substances to help produce the same effect. The most effective turned out to be an alchemically altered gold which proved to be very successful and was in use for many centuries before its secret was lost (called 'shew bread' in the Old Testament).

The energy structures of the gold were altered so that it still looked like gold but was of a very much lighter density. The energy alterations also broke up the molecular bonds and so the gold turned into a powder. The powder was then eaten and the reaction with the digestive system and human energy structures increased psychic potential.

It became clear that there were no simple answers to this energy problem.

Chapter Six

The Removal of The Faerie

To have a chapter titled as this conjures up many images.

How to describe the magnificence of the faerie?

We briefly touched upon the faerie in chapter two and described their role and their origins. That was purely for the purposes of introduction.

The faerie exist as an energy form that was generated by the planet. Their form was originally that of an energy "template". A pure energy that fulfils and resembles its function, a kind of "ghost". Over the centuries, their energy patterns condensed and "solidified" into a more recognisable form, generally as the shapes and forms portrayed in fairy stories. They could become "physical" but only for brief periods and for specific tasks. With Atlantis, that all changed. Atlantis was a testing ground, a place where many forms of life were experimented with. The faerie became fascinated with form and variety and began to take on a more physical structure and density. The addition of density was mainly achieved by Merlin and the Sidhé working together to create an energy gate which could help to enhance and change the energetic makeup of the faerie. This did not make them less faerie, just more solid. These gates are similar in construction to those found at Karnac, Stonehenge, Teoteuhacan etc., but instead of transporting the physical to another world or another place, these gates worked with the energy of the individual and allowed the user to adopt a chosen form and density.

Gates similar to this were the ones first used on Atlantis to achieve a desired change in form that allowed the user to take on characteristics of other forms of life, such as a snake, an ibis, crocodile. etc. It was only when the Atlanteans began to lose some of their higher brain, higher energy, capabilities that manipulation of DNA and solid tissue by more surgical means was required. Use of these gates did not make the faerie fully physical, but gave them an ethereal quality, solid but not solid, energy but not energy. A kind of half way condition which allowed them to easily pass from the world of humanity to the energy realms of the faerie.

In their own way, they mimicked us, but retained their faerie, fay qualities. Try to imagine the way and the feelings of the faerie at this time. They were of the planet, an intrinsic part of what the planet was and is. Into this paradise of life came those with a wish to experiment. These "outsiders" were welcomed with open arms and a great love but, to the faerie, they were a non-permanent part of the planet. If you are an immortal part of that which has been brought into creation, those who borrow your world are only transient.

The faerie did not resent us being here, but they had their ways and responsibilities and we had ours. Our way was to respect and honour the faerie as we also saw ourselves as experimenters who came to play with the energies that this world has to offer. We never saw ourselves as "owners" of the planet. With this respect came an honouring of the faerie as a group of beings who, in our terms, were seen as the planet's "royalty". Strange as this idea sounds, we do not have sufficient words within our vocabulary to describe a combination of honour, love, trust, respect and equality that made up our feelings towards the faerie.

Atlantis was a world shared and all benefited. When the choice to destroy Atlantis was made, the faerie were also involved and they could also see the dangers of what had been created by our mistakes. As protectors of the planet's life, they could not allow for its potential destruction. The faerie did not leave the planet as the humans did, but worked with the planet, alongside Merlin, to limit the harm that the sinking of a continent could do to the planet itself and all of its life.

Whilst Merlin took his rest in Britain and South America, the faerie continued to work with the planet to help restore its balance.

Following Atlantis, some of the Sidhé began to change. They began to take on many more physical characteristics and to adopt a more human density. In other words, they became physical although they retained many of the Sidhé characteristics such as being twelve foot tall. Between Atlantis and the human re-seedings, they shared the Earth with the primate/humans and their faerie brethren who remained between worlds.

When the new humans returned, they accepted the physical Sidhé as a true part of the planet and worked with them in many aspects of human development. In return, the physical faerie helped the new humans understand the ways of the planet and how to work with it in ways beneficial to all. The faerie taught about the plants and animals and helped humanity understand that they needed to work with and protect all animal life.

In very rare instances, the physical Sidhé also mated with humans who produced offspring who contained and encompassed a magical blend of 'angel' and faerie. As humanity began its fall, the Sidhé, temporarily, took over the running of the planet.

By events turning in this way, the Sidhé were given a greater level of respect and where their perceived "regalness" was further enhanced.

The idea of being "kings" did not sit well with the Sidhé as they had difficulty seeing the world in these terms. Although there existed what could be described as a hierarchy within the faerie realms, the levels of existence were a reflection of the differing levels of energy potential that existed between each faerie group and did not represent a "higher" or "lower" individual as we would categorise people.

As human energies began a greater fall, the faerie "kings" (also sometimes called 'Elohim'), the Sidhé, fell into legend and the human/faerie links began to break apart as humanity found greater difficulty in bridging the energy divide. With this process well underway, those who were of the faerie/human "hybrid" maintained a higher level of awareness than the rest of humanity around them. Only a few humans could bridge between the two worlds and, eventually, even these links were only achievable by taking energy enhancing substances such as powdered gold, an alchemical substance whose secrets are only now being rediscovered.

The faerie and humans lived parallel lives with the Sidhé forming the link between both worlds and formed what amounted to a 'kingly' dynasty.

These are the great kings of ancient history. What gave them their position was their ability to span between the worlds of humanity and the world of the faerie to link with the planetary consciousness who maintained all life. Here lies the origins of many belief systems and the root beliefs behind paganism - the link between humans and the faerie and the planet.

In time, a revolution took place and a set of beliefs came into being which were finally cobbled together as Christianity. Christianity is a purely human belief system and came about as a half remembered memory of our off planet origins (created as angels and given use of the planet).

These beliefs led to a great deal of resentment on behalf of a small group of humans and conflicts began to arise, mainly within the humans themselves but also against the Sidhé.

Christianity's aims were of total domination of the planet regardless of how much destruction took place to bring about their ambitions.

With the rise of this organisation, the faerie were put into extreme danger as the Christians would not stop until they had total domination over the planet and all of its life. Their teaching stories about their religion were based upon a creator god and if it became widely known that the planet we lived upon was capable of its own creationary acts, it would totally undermine the message they were attempting to portray. In this respect alone, they would have attempted to destroy the Sidhé.

In the year 538 (in the current calendar), Merlin made a decision. This was made by him alone as he had the ability to stand back and take an overview of the realities of the situation. Merlin removed the Sidhé to a place of safekeeping, away from the destructive potential of this ever growing group of 'Christians'. The Sidhé were removed to a realm of safe keeping away from the planet's direct energy capabilities, into a realm of energy dimensions beyond the human grasp.
At the time, the faerie did not understand this decision and in response, the planet withdrew many of its energies. For ten years, the earth went into decline. The plants began to die and many of the planet's volcanoes erupted as the Earth's energies readjusted to the new situation.

Finally, Merlin persuaded the planet to continue with its nurturing role and a small group of the faerie returned to act on the planet's behalf. These are the faerie that we are more familiar with, the ones who tend our plants and crops.

The energy of the Sidhé has recently been temporarily re-connected to the planet's energies and a change is occurring in the life of the planet, but the time is not yet right for a full return of the faerie. Merlin will act to bring about the faerie's return but only when humanity has let go of its wish for domination and destruction.

Chapter Seven

Merlin, The Celts and Arthur

So, let us try to put all of this together within its context.

Merlin is on Earth to act as its guardian, to provide all of the necessary energies for the development of humanity whilst sustaining the energetic needs of the planet and all of its life whilst the human experiment is running. This is what the Sidhé name Merlin means, 'The Creator of Energy'.

The title of 'Merlin', within the Druidic tradition, originally arose as an honourific title to signify that the most potent 'shaman' in the land had some of the capabilities of the real Merlin. This Merlin became the chief advisor to the Pendragon, the chief of chiefs of the numerous clans of Celtic Britain. In this context, The Merlin acted as a 'seer', a prophet, and chief advisor to the 'King' of Britain.

The Merlin of the Arthurian fantasy was constructed by Geoffrey of Monmouth as an almost evil character, someone who worked in the background to manipulate Kings into carrying out his wishes. By the time that Geoffrey began his story, Britain had long been Roman Christian and the roles played by the Druids had to be shown in a bad light and so the Arthurian Merlin has come to represent all that was bad about pre roman Celtic Britain. His role was softened by the Victorians when they were looking for romantic heroes and what we have ended up with today is an almost anti hero who tried to save the world by protecting Arthur and removing the Druids, a conclusion very far from the truth. Modern interpretations of the Arthurian romance have elevated the Arthurian Merlin's role to an even higher romantic status whilst maintaining Mordred's fictional role as a druidic 'anti christ'.

Whilst Merlin's responsibilities are to the planet as a whole, he took a particular interest in Britain. With the establishment of Atlantis, Britain had taken on the role of being the source of the planet's energies as they arrived from outside the solar system. Silbury Hill was the primary energy receiver and all of the planet's and humanity's energy needs were served through this point. This gave Britain a unique position and the events taking place in Britain which could, at times, determine the future paths of human development.

The time of Arthur in Britain led to changes occurring in the human psyche which had a major influence on the way in which humanity behaved for the next thousand years. This is why so many people find the Arthurian story so appealing and why it has taken on a major significance in recent years. As we develop and change, we have a need to look back in time for indicators, and possibly some heroes, to help us make sense of who and what we are becoming.

The Britain before Arthur was very different to what it is now, even very different to what it was in his time. The low land was covered in forest whilst the higher lands were used for crop growing. The whole economy and way of life was based on agriculture with some mining and metal working. There was sea trade with many lands for some raw materials but most of the trade was of luxury goods or necessary items which could not be manufactured at home. One look at Celtic jewellery design tells us that these were not rustic savages but members of a very sophisticated society with many skills.

Celtic Society

Pre Anglo Saxon Celtic society really is worth taking a closer look at. This is the kind of society which many have aspired to but never really achieved since. The land occupied by each clan was in common ownership. Each individual clan member had the right to farm for food but did not own their particular patch and each member also contributed food to the clan in order that there was always food in time of famine or conflict but also for those members of the clan who could not farm whether by means of age or illness.

They lived under a sophisticated law system where each clan member had stated civil rights. Each person knew precisely what their rights were and any conflicts arising were dealt with by a communal court who arbitrated over the dispute. Criminals were virtually never executed for their transgressions but stripped of their civil rights for a period determined by the court which did not usually exceed three years. During the time of the sentence the 'criminal' worked for the community until such time as the community felt that the crime had been paid. Whilst working in this way, the criminal's family would be fed from the communal food stores to ensure that they did not suffer for the crime of another. When the sentence was completed, the criminal's full rights were restored and they became a full member of the community once again.

All members of the clan were equal and took equal responsibility for their own and the clan's actions. Women could hold any tribal office, including that of chieftain and lead the clan into battle, as with Boudicca. There were laws maintaining the rights of women. When a woman married, the goods she took into the marriage remained hers. She had the right to divorce and there were also special acts of punishment for anyone making attacks upon the person of a woman or upon her honour.

Disputes between clans were also usually settled by arbitration by a council of chieftains. Bloodshed rarely occurred. The strongest act of aggression against a neighbouring clan was to attempt to humiliate them. Each clan had a tree in the centre of their lands which they considered sacred. The worst act of humiliation was for a neighbouring clan to cut down another clan's sacred tree.

If bloodshed or injury did occur, the clans had hospitals to heal the sick or wounded. These were the first hospitals ever developed. There were libraries to record the tribal knowledge and laws. These consisted of 'books' written on wooden stakes or tree bark books in Ogham. It was mainly the Irish clans who developed these libraries as the British Celts had a tradition of memorising and recitation, one of the roles of the tribal 'Merlin' and gave rise to the Celtic bardic traditions.

Chieftains were elected by their clans and only 'ruled' as long as the clan members considered their actions to be for the good of the clan. If a chieftain acted for their own good, the clan would vote them out and choose a new leader. The same applied to the religious leaders, the Druids. They were only in office by the blessing of the clan. Any Druid who acted against the clan or the land was removed from office. This was another aspect of Druidism which the Roman Church took exception to. Their priesthood was a seat of power to be held and maintained at all costs because of the wealth it gave the priest.

The whole of Celtic society was about personal responsibility. By acting in a responsible way, the soul was bettered and all benefited, be that human, faerie, animal, plant or the planet. Whilst there was inevitably bloody conflict between clans, the basis of Celtic society was one of acknowledging the right of self determination and the responsibility that went with that right. The basis for a perfect path to complete the human plan in a short space of time.

People understood the land and its ways. The ways of the seasons and the role played by the many 'spirits' they observed at work within the landscape. There was honour for the land and for the Earth itself, the 'Mother' that gave everything life. This is the source of the Druid beliefs, an understanding of the ways of nature and the Sidhé and faerie who worked with them. An understanding that gave everything life and in return, gave life back to humanity. It is within this cycle of understanding that lay the most immediate way to return to full understanding of the self and full consciousness. This is not to try to present these times as some kind of idyll. Life was very tough, life expectancy was not much beyond fifty and infant mortality was very high. But, it had its merits.

This way of life might, at first sight, appear to be a step backwards. There had been great civilisations established since the destruction of Atlantis. South America, Mesopotamia, Egypt, Greece, etc. had shown that humanity could rise to great heights. But. These civilisations had risen on the knowledge of Atlantis and were, in that respect, very false. This was not humanity rising to these heights but those fresh from other galaxies bringing their knowledge with them and using it to change the Earth, not to work with it. The kind of life described above for the Celtic clans is one where humanity begins to fulfil its chosen task, develop an understanding of the planet and humanity's potential place within the planetary whole. This is what gave it its merit and how it could lead humanity to its chosen goal.

Great buildings and technology have their own merits but they impose human will upon the landscape. They do not lead to understanding of the world or humanity's place within it. These middle civilisations only led to arrogance and this is the main reason for their fall. Man is not here to conquer but to learn and the two approaches are not compatible.

This is, after all, the fundamental purpose for human life, to find a way of fulfilling the human plan. Fifteen thousand years ago we embarked on a journey to find out why Atlantis failed. The only feasible approach to resolve this problem was to work with the earth and all of its life. Ignoring our place within the landscape only leads back to our failure not forward to our understanding and ultimate success.

Other 'Celtic' Cultures

From an historian's point of view, Celtic lands covered Britain, France, Spain and Turkey. This could be considered a very narrow definition of the term 'Celtic'. The dictionary defines a Celt as someone who spoke one of the Celtic languages in the pre Roman west, however, the term could be expanded to include all of the planet's indigenous peoples.

South American, North American, Australian Aboriginal, Alaskan Inuit, Tibetan, Black African, Sumerian, etc. native peoples could all fall under the blanket term of 'Celt' where the term is expanded to its full meaning of those who worked with the land in natural ways, those who honoured the Earth and all of its inhabitants, be that plant, animal or faerie. They all also had their own name for Merlin within their traditions. For example; The Popol Vu, the South American traditional creationary stories, names 'their' Merlin as Zamna.

With the arrival of the energies that allowed for the removal of the free choice of others, many of these natural peoples hid themselves away in the deepest recesses of their lands and away from the conquering hordes. It is in this way that they hoped to preserve the true meaning of human existence and pass it back into human knowledge at the time humanity began its planned reawakening.

Unfortunately, over the past three hundred years, most of those who kept to natural ways, those who maintained the

Human Plan, have been invaded by 'Western' religions and cultures and much of their knowledge and integrity has been forcibly removed and deliberate genocide has prevailed. Almost all of these natural 'Celtic' peoples have been lost and their knowledge and ways of life deliberately and systematically vilified and ignored.

In recent years, those 'Celtic' peoples who have hidden themselves away from the Western destruction, have begun to work within the human mass consciousness to reawaken human understanding of the natural world and have helped us to begin to understand that we have responsibilities towards 'Mother Earth'. This reminding of our selves and our place has helped to fuel the move towards completion of The Plan and humanity, as a whole, is, largely, changing towards its chosen tasks.

Roman and Celtic Christianity

With the decline of the non 'Celtic' civilisations, a new one took their place. Instead of attempting to disseminate the knowledge of humanity's place within the whole, as many of the earlier civilisations had attempted to do, this new empire was based upon conquering and subjugation.

What the Roman Empire represented was a human attempt to move away from its path of learning. The taking over of people's lands and ways of thinking led to a move away from 'The Human Plan' and towards a sense of human supremacy over the Earth. Where man goes, the Earth must follow way of thinking found its beginnings with the rise of The Roman Empire.

The Roman conquest of Britain began in 55 BC with the arrival of Caesar. Despite the revolt led by Boudicca in AD 61, most of England and Wales was under Roman control by the year 84. This only left Scotland, some parts of Wales and

Cornwall to hold out against what the Romans represented. By 143, Hadrian's wall had been completed and the Antonine wall begun. The Celtic tribes in Scotland were being squeezed very hard and it looked as though all of Britain would be conquered.

By the 270's a major expansion had begun and Britain became very Roman in attitude. The new 'middle classes' adopted Roman ways and lived in Roman villas. The population as a whole remained Celtic in their ways and maintained their ways with the land and its spirits but the new 'villa' class adopted Roman religions and although 'pagan' looked to gods who were not of the Earth.

All of this changed when Constantine was made Emperor in 324.

Constantine was something of a renegade as far as Rome was concerned. He rejected Rome as his base and built the city of Constantinople as his capital. He also needed something to support him in his Emperor-ship and looked for a unifying force. In this he discovered the early roots of the Christian church.

Early Christianity had been persecuted by Rome as it could undermine its authority. The true teachings of Jesus the Christ (see chapter nine) were of religious tolerance and a reliance on the self, not on the state - a belief system which fell within the requirements of The Human Plan. However, Constantine seized upon the concept of a new religion as a way of maintaining his authority and bringing the rest of Rome into his control.

Although Christianity is seen as one religion, there are many sub divisions within it. Even by the year 324 there were many different factions who held differing views, many of which were not the views of Jesus but were an amalgam of the many religious views held at the time. What Constantine did at the Council of Nicea in 326 was to establish a new Roman Christianity, one which could be used as a force for domination.

The Roman Emperors had long been seen as a 'God' by their people and it was, therefore, comparatively straight forward for Constantine to take on the role of head of this new religion. What is quite odd about this whole situation is that he gave the running of the new church to Bishops he appointed whilst he remained a non Christian until he converted on his death bed.

After inventing this new Roman Christianity, Constantine imposed it as the official Roman religion where it was rigorously imposed by the new Bishops. As it slowly spread throughout the Empire, it was adopted by the non Roman middle classes of occupied countries and Britain was no exception. By about 400 we have two competing versions of Christianity.

Joseph of Arimathea and the son of Jesus the Christ arrived in Britain in the year 42 and the foundations for Celtic Christianity were laid (see the next chapter). The message brought by Jesus' brother fitted in very well with the Celtic view of the world and an amalgamation occurred between true Christianity and the Druidic beliefs.

Into this christianised Celtic Druidic society came Roman Christianity. There was extreme conflict between the two doctrines and many Celtic Christians travelled to Rome to argue their case, most of which was rejected. Following the Council of Nicea in 326, Celtic Christianity was deemed to be heretical. However, the Celts still attempted to persuade Rome of the error of their ways. One of the most famous Celtic Christian teachers, Pelagius, travelled to Rome in 380 and wrote that he was shocked by the lack of moral standards amongst the Roman clergy. Pelagius' comments on what he found together with his views on the origins of Christianity meant he was excommunicated by Rome and still remains a heretic.

There are many differences between Roman and Celtic Christian beliefs.

The dating of Easter for the Celtic was the first Saturday, their Sabbath, after the first full moon following the Spring Equinox (the Jewish Passover) whilst Rome wanted to avoid any dates coinciding with Jewish festivals as it reminded Christians that Jesus was a Jew. The Celtic church encouraged the participation of the congregation whereas Rome did not. Women were allowed into Celtic monasteries whereas Rome had already developed a distancing from women because of the Mary Magdalene connection. One of the biggest differences was to do with the founding source of the church.

Rome sees Simon Bar-Jonah, 'The Rock', or Saint Peter as its founder whereas the Celtic church sees John son of Zebedee and brother of James as its founder. Given the information from the Dead Sea Community Scroll about the origins of many of the titles given to members of Jesus' community, this would make Joseph of Arimathea, Jesus' brother John, as the Celtic founder of the church, following his visit to Britain in AD 42 and Jesus' father's real name as Zebedee.

Apart from the Church's founder, the other biggest reason for schism was the whole approach to the church's role in the community and how it interacted with its parishioners.

The Celtic Church saw the participation of all of its followers as a fundamental part of its role, nobody was to be excluded from the truth. It saw its role as being within the Celtic sense of responsibility with its main beliefs stemming from the right of everyone to choose and act within that choice whilst retaining the responsibility for those actions. Rome took its role as being dominant over its followers with all of the acts that it took as being ordained by God and if everything is preordained then any action it took was 'God's will'.

The Roman philosophy led to the forcible taking of land and money into its ownership using the concept of pre ordination as its excuse. The Celtic church, on the other hand, did not own any land as it was given by the community for the church's use but remained part of the community.

All in all, fundamental differences which led to major conflict.

Angles, Saxons and Jutes

By about 410, the Roman occupying forces left Britain and Western Europe.

Celtic rule returned and Celtic law was re-established. Many deserted the city states established by the Romans and many of the villa estates were abandoned.

This, unfortunately, was not the end of the story. In 429 Saint Germanus arrived in Britain and started to impose Roman Christianity amongst those who still followed the Roman way of life. Many Celtic Christian sites were desecrated and converted for use by the Roman church.

In addition, the Anglo Saxons and Jutes had been marauding along the Eastern coast of Britain for some time, so much so that even the Romans built massive sea defences against them. With the departure of the Romans, their invasions began in earnest. By about 450 the raids became serious and by 488 all of Kent was under Anglo Saxon rule. By 500 the Anglo Saxons and Jutes occupied as far west as Devon and up to Bristol, the East coast as far North as Whitby. The only regions of England not occupied were parts of East Anglia and London. Even these fell by 538.

There is a great deal of denial, even romanticism over the Anglo Saxon occupation. It is generally considered by some historians that the Anglo Saxons were a peaceful bunch who only came here to trade and settle. Nothing could be further from the truth.

The Angles, Saxons and Jutes were Germanic tribes who considered the Celts to be barbaric. The whole philosophy of these tribes was to gain as much land and wealth as possible at whatever cost. Anyone who stood in the way of their goal was massacred and this is what happened to the Celtic clans.

Archeologically and within the Akashic records, there is no evidence for any intermarrying or the sharing of land. Any Celt who opposed these occupying hordes was put to the sword. The slaughter was wholesale and total. The English massacred the British.

The Anglo Saxon word for the Celts is Welsh, meaning foreigner. The Celtic words for the Anglo Saxon are Sais (Welsh) and Sasenach (Irish and Scots) both still are used to describe the English.

The Death of Arthur

The Celts needed a warlord to try to save their lands and philosophies from the devastating destruction being wreaked by the Anglo Saxon invaders and into this role stepped Arthur. It is immensely ironic that the greatest hero in English folklore was in fact a Celt who tried to destroy the English.

Some things are known about Arthur from historical records, certainly some of his major battles are recorded. The account taken from Lawrence Gardener's book is given in the introduction to this book and there is no doubt that his research fits in with the Akashic accounts except there is one major problem with the dates given by Gardener for Arthur's life as the Akashic is very emphatic about the date of his death and the events that immediately followed.

Archeologically, the historical records have this to say.

Very little is known about the historic Arthur. He was known to be a Celtic Chieftain in the Carlisle area who became Pendragon although some chronicles only describe him as a warlord who fought on behalf of the Pendragon. He fought against the Anglo Saxons but also the occasional marauding band of Irish Celts who attacked the West coast of Britain.

The first battle he led was against the East Angles (of Anglo Saxon) in Lincolnshire around the river Glen. He also then led five other battles in this same region. His seventh battle was around the Scottish borders in the Wood of Celidon against a group of Picts (a northern Celtic clan whose name is Latin and means 'painted ones') and Irish (the Irish Clans were also known by a Latin name, Scotii). His eighth victory is not identified fully although it appears to be for a fortress called Guirmion which is also probably within the Borders region. His ninth victory was in the city of Chester removing an invading Irish Clan (Scotii). His next battle was again in the Borders region against a Pictish Clan around a river called Tribuit. Then he won another battle against the Angles in Rochester.

However, his most famous was the battle of Badon Hill in 516 against the West Saxons (county of Wessex). Historians have placed Badon Hill as now being named Solsbury Hill near Batheaston in Somerset. This victory against the Saxon forces was so decisive that no further Anglo Saxon and Celtic battle is recorded for a further twenty years.

During these battles, Arthur had taken to placing a symbol of the Roman church on his banners and whilst his victories were welcomed by his Celtic compatriots, the Roman symbol was not. This led to huge conflict within the clans where some supported Arthur's leadership whilst others wanted to remain with their Druidic or Celtic Christian beliefs and resented Arthur's leanings towards Rome.

All of this finally came to a head in 538 when forces led by Arthur's son Mordred met Arthur's forces in battle at Camluan on the Scottish borders and both were killed.

The Removal of The Sidhe

The date and outcome of this battle had a major significance as far as all of humanity was concerned. What was lost in this battle was more than just two leaders. Lost here was a whole philosophy and way of life. The Celtic ways could not be sustained without either or both of these men. Arthur because of his battle prowess against the Anglo Saxon invaders and Mordred because of his link with the Sidhé and the ways of the land.

At this point, Merlin acted to place the Sidhé out of the reach of human harm and they were removed to a place of safe keeping where they have remained ever since. Humanity has yet to demonstrate that it is sufficiently ready to deal with their reality.

Merlin acted on his own. Neither the Sidhé nor the planet knew of his plans and both responded to what appeared to be an act of treachery. From Merlin's viewpoint, it was an act to save the Sidhé from the character traits that the Anglo Saxons demonstrated and the way in which the Roman church was imposing its will across Europe. Either of these forces had sufficient impetus and will to destroy the Sidhé because of what the Sidhé represented. The Anglo Saxons because the Sidhé contradicted their gods and they despised the Celts and everything that they represented. The Roman church because the Sidhé represented an act of creation, by the planet, that was not made by their god.

All in all it amounted to the destruction of the Sidhé and, ultimately, the planet as all plant and animal life would be lost if the Sidhé and their faerie workers did not tend to the plants' needs. If they were lost, so would humanity and all life on Earth would cease. The removal of the Sidhé was, ultimately, the greatest change in the history of the Earth since the destruction of Atlantis and the Planet and the faerie responded in a decisive way.

As Merlin had not made his plans clear, the Planet thought that he was acting against it. The Planet's response was to withdraw whilst it considered the new position. In withdrawing, the Planet shrank in size triggering a number of volcanic eruptions. The faerie also withdrew reducing crop production. The result was famine and plague amongst the human population and many died.

It took ten years for the planet to come to terms with Merlin's actions and realise that they were for the overall good and in 548 things began to improve. By then, of course, humanity was well on its way to the path it has taken since and materialism and the Roman view was taking over.

Regardless of the views of others, the Akashic makes it very clear that these events occurred in 538. It is a date of such significance that no matter what other evidence exists, it is in 538 that both Arthur and Mordred were killed. The Akashic is unequivocal about it.

For Merlin, this also meant that his role had changed. Humanity had to be allowed to follow its own path back to understanding and he took on a new role in an attempt to understand the root causes of recent events. Others were to work at awakening mankind to its problems and it could only be man who found their way by themselves.

It has taken nearly fifteen hundred years for humanity to return to the point where it is possible for the Sidhé to return. At the beginning of the twenty first century we are facing the biggest threat to the life on the planet since the bacteria that brought about the destruction of Atlantis, genetically modified plants. If the Sidhé cannot return, all life on the planet has the potential of being destroyed by these organisms and it is the collective will of materialist humanity that is preventing the return occurring.

Chapter Eight

Attempts At Understanding

Something odd had occurred in the human world.

The Universe is constructed of energies which allow for the full range of free choice to be explored. This is the purpose of this Universe, to explore all of the possibilities available when all is freely available.

This freedom to choose also extends to Earth.

No one, throughout the whole of the Universe has the right to remove the free choice of others. Yet a situation had arisen on Earth where several groups appeared to be doing so. This deliberate removal of choice had only occurred once within the whole of Universal history and that was caused by the accidental mixing of genes from predatory animals on Atlantis. This new threat was something entirely different and, somehow, the reasons for this fundamental change in behaviour had to be found. Merlin's role is to be the "guardian" of the Earth, if these individuals and groups continued in this way, the Planet's role and integrity could fall under attack and as guardian, Merlin had to act.
But where was Merlin to start?

The first signs of a change in behaviour had begun with Alexander The Great. Societies had developed in their own ways, some good and some not so good. There had been border conflicts in the past and certainly there had been ideological conflicts but no one had attempted to take over the lands of others on the scale seen with Alexander.

Alexander was finally defeated by his own men but it had opened the doors for others to take on the impetus, the energies, for this kind of change in human behaviour.

Directly following Alexander came the beginnings of the rise of The Roman Empire and ultimately the Roman Church. The Angles, Saxons and Jutes then followed and most of the advancing world was in conflict.

The Celtic societies in the west and the Middle East communities acting under the tutelage of Jesus the Christ and his followers should have begun to merge, drawing with them all of the peoples in between. This merging should have shown the way to complete The Human Plan by about the end of the first or second century. Instead of completion, we now had conflict which deliberately attempted to remove Celtic and true Christian understanding.

There was something very odd about this change of energies. Since the founding of the Roman Empire, there had been a noticeable change in human aspirations.

The Human Plan, formulated by Merlin fifteen thousand years ago, provided a framework into which humanity could begin to learn its lessons in how to regain its lost higher levels of consciousness. With the commencement of the knowledge gathering process, Karma, seven thousand years ago, humanity had begun in earnest to unravel the secrets to life on Earth. The process had been slow as there had been a great deal to learn but the rise of the Celtic societies across much of Europe who worked with the land and the establishment of the Sumerian, and later Egyptian, 'scientific' approaches to understanding as well as the Greek mathematical and philosophical explorations, The Plan was moving forwards.

By about 500 BC we have human societies moving rapidly forwards into understanding themselves and their world around them. Despite the occasional bloody conflict, the world was working towards its goal.

Then, something began to change. It began with small groups attempting to take over other people and other regions. This was not part of The Plan.

This Universe is based upon a collection of energies that affords every individual the absolute right to complete freedom of choice but it does not allow the freedom of choice to forcibly remove the choice of others. Taking away the choice of others was now occurring and the cause had to be found if humanity was to stay on the planet.

As The Roman Empire spread, rapidly followed by the Angles, Saxons and Jutes and then several others with empire building aspirations, especially the Roman Church, freedom to choose was being rapidly and bloodily removed. The reasons for this change had to be found or all was lost.

The Hunt for Answers

The Human Plan was, essentially, very simple. The realisation that the base energy frequencies of the Planet itself was sufficient to slow down human higher brain functions meant that if the 'experiment' of Earth was to be fulfilled, a way needed to be found to work with these dense frequencies to bring humanity back to its full potential. The Human Plan was just that, a method by which all would take on aspects of physical life and the gathered knowledge would form part of the mass consciousness, the Akashic. As more and more information was added, the way to return to containing the whole of the consciousness in a physical body could be found and the paradise of Earth would be regained.

A great deal of work had been achieved and many avenues of approach had been explored. Two thousand five hundred years ago we were in a position where we could begin the final stages of our plan. As the direction of human life began to change these final stages were put on hold. Were these new energy frequencies, the ones which allowed the removal of choice, an aspect of the completion of the plan? Were they a new twist to the Planet's unique energy structures or were they an entirely new range of frequencies that were part of a Creationary act?

At this stage there were no answers and it took many hundreds of years to finally track the problem down.

Merlin travelled back to The Thirteen to see if they could shed some light on the problem. As those who maintain the balance of energies within the Universe, if there had been a change of energies on a fundamental level, they would know. Their answer was they had no knowledge of deliberate change and assumed that it must be an aspect of the planet or something within humanity itself.

Armed with this answer Merlin returned to Earth. What to do next? Without knowing the answer to this problem The Human Plan could not be completed. If the Plan could not be completed the Earth could be lost because humanity's actions with these new energies would eventually take them to the point where they would force complete control of the planet and its life.

Was the way forward the complete removal of humanity or was there a way to find the answer? After discussions on continuing with the Planet's consciousness and a wish to contain the problem on Earth, instead of unleashing these energies into the rest of the Universe, the solar system gates were sealed and Merlin took the decision to live a series of human lifetimes to try to establish the root cause of the problem.

Initially, the course Merlin took was that of adult 'birth'. If the consciousness is intact and functioning as one, many things are possible that are not possible when in full human form. One of these possibilities is that of regenerating the body into a newer or different structure. In this way, Merlin effectively lived for nine hundred years in one 'lifetime'.

This process allowed for the investigation of several aspects of human experience. It is a question of adopting the variety of densities of energies to produce the human body. Once the experiences of one body were complete, it was a question of dissolving those energies, in other words, moving out of the 'physical' and back into the energetic form and then reusing the denser energies to form a new adult body. Adult birth in a form necessary to carry out the chosen task. These forms could be male or female or of any of the racial groups which make up the mass of humanity.

In order to try to understand the new energies humanity had taken on board, Merlin felt this was the correct approach. By maintaining full conscious awareness, he could communicate freely with the world around him, the mass consciousness and others of the universal civilisations who were working within The Human Plan. It was also possible to act very quickly. If a situation arose which could possibly begin to unravel the problem, Merlin could regenerate and take on new form without having to go through the normal birth process.

His first course of action was to look at some who were newly affected by these energies.

The Greek Empire

It is at this time that the other 'great' culture began to rise and take on some elements of Roman empirical ideas and this was Greece. Greece also began to expand and try to form its own empire.

Another empire was beginning to rise within all of these conflicts who had the potential to stop both assaults on reason and this was Persia (Sumeria). The Persian leaders were a middle ground. Not as 'advanced' as the Celts and Jesus Christians but they were certainly not the force for destruction that the Romans, Germans and Greeks were. The Sumerians were the cradle of the post Atlantis world. It is from the original Sumerian lands that the sources of much of our understanding of the world, science and medicine, stems. In the intervening centuries they had become a little lost and dispossessed but were now attempting to come to humanity's aid. This is where Merlin began.

In order to begin to understand the need to conquer, it was felt that a good place to start was to take on the would be conqueror head on. Merlin took on board a human form resembling a Persian in middle age and in 599 led the Persian forces into battle against the Greeks.

The Greeks had always been seen as the 'intellectuals' of the world and had usually only interacted with other cultures by means of trade, either of ideas or of goods. They had been generally peaceful but began to take on imperialist leanings. Not all Greeks wanted to take this line as they favoured trade to conflict. However, there was a mood for change and the Greek armies, led by the general Themistocles, were forced into expanding the Greek borders. Themistocles was not in favour of this expansionist programme and looked for ways to return Greece to its more peaceful existence. However, the mood of the people was for war and he led the Greek forces on several successful campaigns.

The Persians were attempting to halt this advance. The Romans, at this time were busy fighting amongst themselves and the Germanic tribes on their Northern borders and so were not particularly interested in the conflicts of the Greeks or the Persians.

Merlin took on the name of Xerxec and met the Greek general, Themistocles. The Greeks won the battle and, potentially, changed the course of world history. Had the Persians won, the world would have, potentially, changed course. As it was, the Greeks became more trade orientated and moved away from their more intellectual pursuits. The Persians slowly slipped into oblivion.

From this point on, humanity changed and a flood of new energy swept the globe.

The whole of human society, apart from a few small enclaves, switched from The Human Plan into the pursuit of power and wealth. Human society would never be the same again. The decision to remove the Sidhé had at least been vindicated but humanity was, to all intents and purposes, lost.

Merlin pops up in a number of locations under many different guises taking on many roles for the next nine hundred years. Virtually all of these 'lifetimes' remain unrecorded as it is one 'soul' moving through time and place and the Akashic only notes Merlin and not the various names. What is known is that he worked a great deal with groups who were attempting to disseminate knowledge of the true Human Plan to the population as a whole. One such group was The Knights Templar and Merlin's work with them is covered in the next chapter.

By about 1340, Merlin decided to take another step. The nine hundred years since the removal of the Sidhé had not brought his understanding any further forward. Despite taking on many human appearances at many locations around the globe, no answers were forthcoming. The reasons for humanity's change of direction had not been found. The answers could not be found in the mass consciousness, nor in Merlin taking direct action against those who appeared to have somehow taken on these strange energies. Could the answer lie in being entirely physical? There was only one way to find out.

For a little while, Merlin rested and watched.

Human Lives, Human Choices

By the time Merlin decided to rest, some of his actions, taken with several groups, began to show fruition with the start of what is known as The Renaissance. Renaissance comes from a latin word, rinascere, meaning reborn. This rebirth had the potential to drag humanity back on track and bring new meaning to human lives. For a while Merlin watched developments to see how far this change of ideas would go. Eventually he decided to take an active role and underwent birth in Caprese near Florence in 1475 where he was named Michelangelo Buonarroti.

As a child he learned painting but moved to sculpture. He became popular locally and was sponsored by a Templar family, the Medicis in Florence, where he also worked with the other great Templar scholar of his time, Leonardo Da Vinci. When he moved to Rome he came to work with Pope Julius 11 and later Pope Paul 111. Moving in these circles, Merlin (Michelangelo) had access to the most powerful members of human society. The power and wealth of the Medici family opened many doors for him and his relationships with the two Popes gave him unique access to the inner workings of the Vatican. Where better to learn about the sources and uses, especially abuses, of power?

Another major change had also occurred one year after his birth with William Caxton inventing the printing press. Prior to this invention, all books had been reproduced by hand. This made them extremely expensive and inaccessible to the vast majority of people. It also meant that the church had an effective monopoly on reading, writing and knowledge as most book copying was carried out by monks. Knowledge only came to the majority of people through what the church told them which was usually a distortion of the truth and very often fabrication to suit the church's propaganda.

With the printing press, books could be produced comparatively cheaply and the dissemination of knowledge and ideas could be spread all over the globe. A true potential rebirth for all of mankind.

By 1564 Merlin (Michelangelo) had become a little disillusioned with life and he left his physical body to attempt another approach. Although his life as Michelangelo had provided many answers and certainly a great deal of understanding of the human condition, there were still no pointers to the source of the change of energies.

During his time as Michelangelo, Merlin began to realise that the answer did not lay with living with the powerful in one location. Whilst, as an artist, he had become powerful himself and had major influence over those around him, this was a power that came from achievement whilst those for whom he worked had achieved power by a different means. Their power lay partly in the wealth of their families but also in some way which could not be defined. The Vatican also had great power but that had come from taking choice from others. How could power be taken? This was the question at the crux of his search and he was no closer to finding the answer. To further extend his range of search, he made use of a capability which all of us have made use of over our numerous lifetimes, multidimensionality.

Multidimensionality is a process by which the consciousness, the total soul, divides itself into more than one. To live a human lifetime requires about one quarter of the total capability of the consciousness. This leaves three quarters as the 'higher self'. By producing another physical being from the residue of the soul, it has been possible to live a concurrent or overlapping life in order to make more efficient use of the time we had available to complete the human plan, see *The Journey Home*.

The percentages are variable. Some life choices require more than twenty five percent whilst others require less. Sometimes we have varied the percentages during a particular life time, childhood and old age can be times where the percentage of total consciousness in the body can be less than during adolescence and mid adult life. For example; if one life is approaching old age, a child can be born with a greater percentage of the total consciousness by drawing away from the one who no longer requires their full faculties, with an infinite variety of variations available to suit the individual circumstances.

At two minutes past four in the afternoon on the thirteenth of July 1527, a multidimensional aspect of Merlin was born in Greenwich in London. His father was Roland Dee who was a 'gentleman sewer' to the court of Henry VIIIth and based at Greenwich Palace, the main residence of Henry. Merlin's new name was John Dee.

Growing up in Henry's court at one of the most turbulent times of history gave Dee (Merlin) a unique perspective on how power can be used and abused.

With Henry breaking away from Rome, his court was filled with spies and intrigue, power plays and alliances. As a servant's son, he had almost total access to the games played and who the major players were. He also began to learn how such power struggles were fought and how to set such games into motion, something that would stand him in good stead in future years. Following an education at Chelmsford Grammar School, he entered St John's College Cambridge in 1542 to study mathe-matics and the sciences.

Given the Vatican block on any scientific study, Henry's Reformation meant that this was the first time that such courses were available in Britain.

Dee excelled himself at these subjects and become a major scholar graduating in 1547 where he then was appointed a Fellow of Trinity College and an Under-Reader in Greek. It was whilst at Trinity that he first showed his abilities as a thinker and 'engineer'.

In 1548 he left Cambridge and moved to Louvrain near Brussels. Whilst colleges in Britain were beginning to offer courses in previously banned subjects, the Low Countries had much more advanced college courses and a greater freedom to explore the possibilities such subjects had to offer. From here, he travelled around Europe meeting as many scholars as possible and gave several influential lectures.

By now Henry had died and the crown was held by Edward VI, who Dee was presented to in 1551 on his return to England. On his return Dee worked for several people, particularly Lord Northumberland who was the 'spy master' of the English court.

With his new role, Dee began to develop encryption codes for messages sent to the numerous English spies both at home and abroad. Some of these codes have only been broken this century using the most powerful decoding computers whilst some of his written works have defeated even these methods and remain unread.

By now Mary had taken over the throne and attempted to undo many of Henry's reforms. Whilst Dee had not expressed any religious preferences, his spying activities led him into conflict with the new court and in 1553 he was imprisoned in the tower. His imprisonment did not last long however, and he secretly began to develop his interests in all things 'magic'.

The use of the term magic does not imply any dark goings on but the investigation of how to obtain information. These investigations mainly took the form of working with various mediums. However, his secret came out and he was once again imprisoned, this time for the charge of 'conjuring'.

In 1559, Elizabeth was crowned and his fortunes once again changed and he was appointed an unofficial consultant to the court on matters of science, astronomy and astrology, he also maintained his role within Elizabeth's spy network.

He became a firm favourite of the Queen and she visited his home in Mortlake on very many occasions both to consult with him and visit as a friend. She had a great interest in his work and commissioned several books from him on various associated subjects.

In 1582 Dee meets with a 'skryer' called Edward Kelly. Kelly was not considered a trustworthy character but, nevertheless, he somehow persuaded Dee that he was genuine and became Dee's medium for many years.

Dee had already began his work with 'Angelic' sources and Kelly now took over as intermediary. By taking the route of using a medium to contact those considered to be of the 'Angelic' realms, Dee (Merlin) hoped to investigate several directions at the same time.

Dee was very close to the Queen of England and many who held great power both in Britain and Europe, by also working with those who were non-physical, he hoped to gain knowledge and information from as many different sources as possible.

At the request of the English court, mainly for spying purposes or to establish new alliances for the crown, Dee and Kelly travelled through Europe to Krakow and Prague to contact the Emperor Rudolph of Bohemia and King Stephen Bethany of Poland. Whilst in Poland, Dee and Kelly began investigating Alchemy.

Alchemy has earned a notoriety for its practitioners' attempts at transmuting base metals, or other substances into gold. In reality, the Alchemist's role was to discover the route the soul should take to return to regain full consciousness. In other words, transmuting base metal, the low level of human conscious awareness, into gold, the highest level of human consciousness. Experiments were carried out on base metals to see if it was possible to develop an 'elixir' capable of carrying out this task, commonly known as the 'Philosopher's Stone'.

However, Dee and Kelly were having difficulty with the Roman church who persuaded Emperor Rudolph that Dee's work was 'develish' and his books were burned and Dee and Kelly banished from Bohemia.

In 1586 Dee, Kelly and both their families, arrived in a small Bohemian town called Trebon. Under the patronage of the local ruler, Vilem Rozmberk, they finally settled and continued with both their alchemical and channelled work.

Surprisingly, Kelly became very successful at creating gold and this led to conflict between himself and Dee. In 1587 Kelly broke away from Dee and eventually died in prison. Dee eventually returned to England and his son, Arthur, took over the mediumship work from Kelly.

Despite all of these endeavours and hardships, Dee (Merlin) was no closer to understanding the problems he was investigating. There were energies at work which could not be understood but the consequences of these energies were disrupting all the progress humanity was making. The power to take away freedom of choice was proving devastating in its effects but its source was proving impossible to find.

Dee finally died in November 1608, a very frustrated man.

From this point onwards, Merlin took on a series of human lifetimes that ranged from rich to poor, male to female in an attempt to find some clues but all failed.

The Akashic is a little unclear about these lives as they were deliberately intended to be as other 'normal' humans lived them. Whilst all lives are recorded in the Akashic, with Merlin disappearing into the mass of humanity, the threads of his lives are not easy to follow.

There are, nevertheless, some glimpses. Life as a vagrant living rough in the forests of Czechoslovakia: life as a woodsman in Germany: life as a fisherman in Sicily: a spinster in an English parish.

These were lifetimes lived in ways in which any ordinary person would live their lives and it is only within the twentieth century that the thread of the true Merlin can be picked up again and then only by the actions taken to assist mankind to re-find its way.

Author's Note

The use of the term 'Angel' is one which many have taken to mean an emissary from God and have, therefore, taken channelled messages from these sources to be 'of truth'. It is worth noting that from my many years of investigating these beings, there are three sources from which this belief springs. The first is the religious indoctrination which has spread over the centuries, particularly through the Christianised world. In the Old Testament, there are many mentions of a hierarchy of angels led by four archangels. With the publication of the Community Scroll from the Dead Sea Scrolls, it is clear that this hierarchy is nothing more than titles given to the priests and high priests of the Jewish church.

There are three branches of the priesthood here given in their order of rank: Zadock, Abiathar and Levi. Each of these orders have their High Priest who also takes on the title of messenger. The title of messenger is usually expressed in its Greek form i.e. aggelos or angelos (Latin angelus). In other words, the word 'angel' means messenger and the word 'archangel' means chief messenger. In terms of the priesthood, the High Priests take on the name of the first chief messengers to hold these offices, as recorded in The Book of Enoch. In this way the High Priest of the order of Zadock becomes Archangel Michael, the High Priest of Abiathor becomes Archangel Gabriel and the High Priest of the order of Levi becomes Archangel Sariel. In addition to this, the Levi priesthood has a division which has a chief priest and his official title is the Archangel Raphael.

The Book of Enoch is an ancient text about seven thousand years old which is a work of the Jewish Mysteries, the Cabbala. This is one of the first books to set out the roles and functions of the priests within the Jewish faith. It lists all of the 'angels' in order of hierarchy, more correctly, it lists all of the orders of priests.

In this way, the four Archangels to which many refer or claim to channel, only exist as part of a priesthood hierarchical tradition rather than a godly emissary and fall into the second category.

116

The second source of angelic knowledge comes from those who are not in a physical form i.e. those who are not living a physical lifetime on Earth but are between lives. These souls attempt to help those who are living by passing on information they have gained either whilst alive or since they left their bodies and connected with their total consciousness. These messengers also include those from other worlds who also have a desire to assist mankind reach its goal. Given humanity's religious expectations, many of these beings will take on the persona of an archangel or angel as this is what the channeller is anticipating. This is not usually an attempt to mislead but an attempt to meet the channeller's expectations.

The third source of these beliefs stems from the fact that humanity has travelled so far from its original levels of consciousness that it does not recognise when it is speaking to its higher self. The energies contained within the total consciousness are immense and seen from the human perspective can appear to be another person rather than the remainder of the soul that they are. Given the religious expectations mentioned above, the higher self can be assumed to be an angelic source.

With the source of the problem Merlin was attempting to track down finally revealed in the twenty first century, it appears as though many of those he attempted to contact as Dee were affected and some of the information channelled to him through Kelly was fundamentally flawed and intended to lead Dee in the wrong direction or confuse him to a point where he could not make sense of some of the information he was given.

Chapter Nine

Merlin and the Knights Templar

The Knights Templar have a history shrouded in mystery, myth and legend almost as much as Merlin himself. Whilst there has been a resurgence of knowledge of, and interest in, the Templars in recent years, their history begins at a much earlier time than most realise. Their story really begins in old testament times with the migration from Sumeria of those we know as the Tribes of Israel.

This can only be a very brief history of world events as it is given in order to put the Templars into an historical context in how they relate to Merlin. However the full history of these peoples is well worth investigating as they run a thread through the whole of human history in the last two and a half thousand years.

With the destruction of Atlantis, those who became modern man began again. As previously mentioned, this was twenty thousand years ago and the regions newly "colonised" were South America, Mesopotamia, Egypt, a region which encompassed Britain, Ireland and Northern France, Tibet and Southern Greece. All of these repopulated areas carried memories of Atlantis and each person was a fully integrated consciousness. Each of these groups worked, experienced, experimented and developed in their own ways but all communicated openly with every other group.

To describe what it felt like to have all of our consciousness in the body is not something which our vocabulary is capable of expressing. As an example. A shark has sensory systems which are very different to our own. It has a series of sensory organs down its flanks which can detect the movement of an object in the water up to several meters away. It can detect the fluctuations of the Earth's magnetic lines of force and can navigate by the lines. It can detect the presence of one drop of blood in the water from a distance of up to three miles. The only way of understanding these sensory perceptions is to become a shark but, once you did that, you could not communicate what the additional senses felt like as they are such a fundamental part of the shark that they could not be separated or put into a language which a human could understand.

The same is true for the awareness and additional perceptions we would have when we regain full consciousness.

As the energies of the consciousness began their anticipated slowing, each group began to develop their own ways of communicating amongst themselves but the first to develop a written form were those who were in Mesopotamia and so, about fifteen thousand years ago, the first form of writing appeared. It is because of these written records that the Sumerians are credited with the discovery of healing techniques although in reality all of the groups had the same skills, it is just the written records of these peoples that have survived. The earliest form of writing is of vertical lines forming consonants with horizontal or diagonal crossing lines differentiating the letters and this is why Hebrew, Ogham and Runes are very similar, they stem from the same root. This period is also the time where religions have their root. As the consciousness slowed, teaching stories were developed so that we could remember our origins and place ourselves into a greater context. As we further slid from total consciousness, these stories took on an air of myth and individuals began to add, remove or embellish stories for their own purposes and the true meaning of humanity has, largely, been lost. Written records of these stories were made and some have been found by modern day archaeologists but as they are now so far removed from the current religious stories they are usually ignored or categorised as myth stories from a primitive peoples.

From Sumeria, this group spread to join with their counterparts in all lands but particularly with those in Egypt. As they worked with the Egyptians, these people became fully integrated into their new lands and became a part of the Egypt we know through history (although the story is far from fully told and many extremely important aspects have been totally omitted from historical research). Eventually, a group were expelled from Egypt under the leadership of the ousted pharaoh Akhenaten who became known by the Egyptian word for 'true' (in terms of being the heir), Meses which is pronounced Moses.

The Brotherhood of Sion

In the departure from Egypt, Moses was accompanied by Jacob and a group of Hebrews. The word Hebrew means 'chosen ones' as they travelled with the true pharaoh. On their departure from Egypt, they took with them most of the writings that a pharaoh would only have access to and these formed the basis of The Cabbala. This "secret" knowledge was known as "The Tables of Testimony" and was contained within The Ark of the Covenant. The 'Tables of Testimony' were the records of Atlantis and are discussed later in this chapter. The Ark of the Covenant was the 'box' built to contain the Tables and generated its own electrical charge large enough to electrocute anyone attempting to open it without the knowledge of how to open it properly.

They finally settled in Canaan (Palestine). During this period, they began to break up into various factions that became the tribes of Israel until they eventually settled their differences and became united under the first king, Saul, in about 1055 BC. Saul's son in law expanded the territory occupied by the Jewish tribes to include Jerusalem and succeeded to the throne as King David. David was followed by his son, Solomon, and a great period of enlightenment began. Solomon was renowned for his wisdom, most of which came from access to the information brought with Moses out of Egypt. Solomon amassed a huge fortune and brought together all of the information carried by his peoples and these were placed together with the Ark of the Covenant under the Temple in Jerusalem.

With the death of Solomon around 960 BC, the kingdom broke apart and a number of factions fought for control until about 720 BC when the region was invaded by the Assyrians. This led to a period of persecution and the peoples were finally banished back to Mesopotamia by Nebuchadnezzar in about the year 650 BC. Following about seventy years in captivity, they moved back to Jerusalem. It is at this time that several events occurred which led to the eventual forming of the Knights Templar. There were also events taking place on a universal level which had an immense bearing on the way in which humanity acted and these are covered in chapter ten.

Upon their return to Jerusalem, there were essentially two factions. The first were the priests who were attempting to take control of the people and bring power to themselves. It was at this time that the Old Testament began to be written and much of the tribes' history was brought together in these books. In addition to the history, a set of rules began to be formulated as a way of bringing power to the priests and away from the structure of kingdoms. This was not only a means of gaining control by the priests but of attempting to unite the ten tribes together and stopping the many squabbles and bloody conflicts.

During this time of resettlement and consolidation there grew another group of people who had the same ideals of unification in mind but wanted to take another route. A dynasty had been established through Saul, David and Solomon (a Sidhé blood line) and they saw the best way of unifying the people was through the reestablishment of the kingdom. This group took on the name "The Brotherhood of Sion" and it is from this brotherhood that the Knights Templar were brought into being almost 1500 years later.

The "treasure" of Solomon had been deposited under the Temple for safe keeping. It had been hidden in an energy "vault" which had a time lock. The knowledge of how to construct such vaults had been contained in The Tables of Testimony and involved making the object to be hidden slip in time by up to two seconds. Two seconds does not sound like very much but it is sufficient to remove objects from a current reality. In other words, the hidden object no longer exists in the current time, rendering it invisible and non physical. The key to the lock is a sound, a single note, which sets up a resonance within the surrounding space, creating a vibration which brings the vault back to its current time. It is also possible to move the observer through the time slip and out of current time. For example, gates into the Templar energy grid and secret sites have guardians, knights from various times, who exist within a time slip. These time slips remove them physically from their own time and hold them in a state of non time where they do not age or require food.

The origin of the name Templar stems from this root. Although they were involved with the Temple of Solomon, their name does not derive from the temple but from an ability to generate time slips (latin - tempus).

The Brotherhood of Sion knew of the existence of the vault and the knowledge it contained but had forgotten how to open it. For this purpose, they called upon Merlin to assist them in their goal. Their plan was to access the Tables of Testimony and freely disseminate the information amongst the people and bring about a period of change, a beginning of the return of the full consciousness into the physical body. This is, after all, the purpose of Karmic experience, to learn how to integrate the whole consciousness into the physical body. After almost five thousand years of humanity struggling to re-find itself, it was considered time to begin a more direct approach.

The legacy of the Davidic dynasty was the hope of a "King", an individual who could reunite people into a single humanity with free access to the knowledge of the truth about humanity's origins. With such a group of people intact, they would travel to other regions of the world and assist others in their own transitions to full consciousness integration. A high ideal, but one which had strong possibilities of success.

A process of slow education was begun. The information was copied in a very much watered down version and distributed, secretly, to teachers, Cabalists and alchemists to begin introducing the basic principles of the plan. Once the priests discovered what was happening, they began attempting to prevent any further spread of the concepts and numerous problems resulted.

The Birth of Jesus The Christ

These factions remained opposed to each other delaying the whole process until a new opportunity arose to put the Brotherhood's intentions into reality. In 6 BC a child was born which brought together several of the important and necessary bloodlines. This child we know as Jesus the Christ (Christos is a Greek word meaning "King").

Jesus' parents were well connected within the social structures of the time and could move freely between both of the main faction groups. Jesus' birth also fulfilled many of the predictions (prophecies) for the return of a 'King of the Jews'.

This is the true reality of Jesus and his life's purpose. The unification of the old kingdom and the reunification of the consciousness within the physical body. However, he was born into a time of conflict where his kingdom was under the control of occupying forces in the form of the Romans and where his own people could not decide on the direction their lives should take. The people were looking for a leader, someone from the line of David who could lead them out of their predicament and fulfil the old prophesies. This is what Jesus became, a "freedom fighter" as well as a teacher. Once the Romans had been removed and the kingdom re-established, Jesus could take on his primary role of a teacher and humanity could begin their needed change.

There are huge inconsistencies and fabrications surrounding the life and times of Jesus. Many are due to a misunderstanding of the religious practices and customs of the religious group that Jesus' parents belonged whilst others are a fabrication to suit the political aspirations of the Roman emperor Constantine and subsequent Bishops of Rome.

Joseph and Mary belonged to the tribe of Judah which placed them within the dynastic blood line of David. They were also known as Nozrim, or to put it into its biblical context, Nazarenes. Nozrim is a shortening of a hebrew word meaning 'Keepers of the Covenant', the designation of the peoples who lived at Qumran where the Dead Sea Scrolls were found. This is the origin of the idea that Jesus was of the town of Nazareth. Nazareth is now a suburb of Jerusalem but it does not appear on any map until after the Romans sacked Jerusalem in 70 AD and an encampment of the Nazarenes was formed a little way away from the city.

The Nozrim had a number of very strict rules governing their lives so to illustrate how so many of the Christian concepts arose we can take a look at one important aspect of the community, their customs surrounding marriage and conception.

A man and woman would become betrothed and three months later a First Marriage would take place in September which began a formal 'espousal'. The husband and wife would remain celibate until early December. During this period she was known as an 'almah', this is a hebrew word meaning 'young woman' and frequently mistranslated to mean 'virgin'. In this way, all Nozrim births were 'virgin' births. If she became pregnant during this first December, a formal Second Marriage would take place three months into the pregnancy. If she did not become pregnant, relations would be suspended until the following December when the couple would again try to conceive. During both the First and Second marriage ceremonies, the bride would anoint her husband's feet with the oil spikenard and then wipe away the oil with her hair. This would be the normal course of marriage and this form of anointing with this particular oil did not occur for any other purpose.

It would appear that Joseph and Mary did not quite follow this formal sequence of events and began the more intimate part of their marriage a little sooner than custom allowed. With Mary's pregnancy beginning a little out of sync with the normal sequence, the intervention of the priests was required. The priests sanctioned the First Marriage and conception and the Second Marriage was allowed to proceed and their child, Jesus, was given an official birthday in September, his actual birth taking place in March.

The same ceremonial sequence was followed some thirty six years later when Jesus married Mary Magdalene to continue the royal dynastic line.

Within this community, there was a strict hierarchy of priests, each with their own traditional title. The highest line of priests were known as Zadok whilst the second in line were the Abiathar and the third was Levi. These priests were officially designated as 'messengers of God'. The word used for messenger in several ancient languages is Angel. Therefore, the official title of the Zadok priest is Archangel Michael whilst the official title of the Abiathar priest is the Archangel Gabriel and the Levi priest was Archangel Sariel. There is a full list of the hierarchy of the priests within the community contained in the First Book of Enoch. All of these names arose from the first holders of these titles when the records of the community were written. In this way, the first priest to hold the highest office was called Michael, the priest who was second in importance was called Gabriel and so on down through the priestly levels.

In addition to these 'named' titles, they also carried other official titles within the overall community. In this way, the Zadok priest was 'Father', the Abiathar priest was 'Son' and the Levi priest 'Spirit'. Those who were members of the community followed the 'Way' and were deemed to be 'The Children of Light'. Within the community there was also an official 'opposition' who tested the followers of the 'Way' in their adherence to their beliefs and official customs, this 'opposition' was designated 'The Forces of Darkness' and the head of this department was the Chief Scribe known as 'Accuser'.

In addition to the priests, other titles were the tradition within the tribal community to denote particular "rank". The name Joseph was the official title of the next in the line of succession to the Davidic kingly line. Therefore, Jesus' father was not actually baptised as Joseph but was known as 'Joseph' through his ancestry. With Jesus seen as being the true 'King' within this succession, the title of 'Joseph' passed to his brother, John, on their father's death. So, brother John became 'Joseph' and was also the 'Crown Prince' or, to give him his full official title, Joseph of Arimathea.

It is also worth noting the normal course of events following pregnancy and birth within this community. There were extremely strict rules that had to be adhered to as far as the relationships between men and women were concerned. Within the community, women held equal status to men with their own hierarchy of priestess titles. Within marriage there were also a number of titles denoting a woman's official status. An unmarried woman was called 'young woman'. When she became betrothed, she retained this title until she and her husband had completed their Second Marriage and she had given birth. If the child was female, the couple could not have further marital relations for three years. If the child was male, this period of celibacy was extended to six years. Once she had given birth, the woman was officially designated as 'mother', when she and her husband began their period apart, her status was changed to 'widow' and she was expected to shed tears for her 'lost' husband. During the period of celibacy, the men lived in what was effectively a monastery and the women in a similar establishment. In order to ensure that the rules of strict celibacy were adhered to, the Chief of the Scribes (of the Forces of Darkness) had the official function of keeping husbands and wives apart from each other, in this task he took on the title of 'Accuser' or, in Hebrew, 'Satan'.

Throughout the Akashic, the only reference to a title of this type is this human made variety. The only 'evil' in the world comes from man, not from outside forces. The concept of a 'devil', an evil force, is entirely man made.

Jesus was born into a community with strict rules controlling all aspects of life and many of the individuals within the community had some kind of official title. There were also very strict rules governing behaviour and all activities, all of which had official titles and forms of language to describe them. It is the language of the community which has given rise to so many misinterpretations of the life of Jesus and his performance of apparent 'miracles'.

The information given above about the times and traditions of the community Jesus was born into has only been given to provide background information and to put much of what has followed into context. The New Testament version of events does actually provide much of this information, it has just been misinterpreted to suit a particular doctrine.

A Route to Change?

Jesus was a catalyst for change and a person who generated a huge amount of opposition from the priests of all of the tribes but also within his own community. His concept of change and the steps needed to reunite all of the Jewish tribes brought about an appeal from some within his own community for his death.

The story of the crucifixion is another one which many have challenged and much of accepted 'truth' is no more than a further misinterpretation of how the story of the events has been written. There are two schools of thought on the actual events of the time. The first is that the 'sponge filled with vinegar' given to Jesus also contained a combination of herbs which could induce a state resembling death. All 'medicines', herbal remedies, of the time were preserved in vinegar. The second is that Jesus was not crucified at all but his place on the cross was taken by Simon the Cyrene. In reality, a huge subterfuge was enacted which put Jesus on to the cross but allowed him to be taken down very much alive. The important aspect of the story is that Jesus did not die on the cross and there are a number of accounts from other traditions which accurately place him in various locations at dates following his claimed death on the cross.

One thing was certain, Jesus could not remain in Palestine. The knowledge of his survival soon became common knowledge and he was pursued by both the priests and the Romans. From this point, Jesus began his travels to many other lands and spread the ideals and knowledge he held to many people.

In the mean time, his brother John took on the role of protector of Jesus' wife and son as well as spreading the teachings of The Tables of Testimony. In these two roles, he travelled to Marseilles in Southern France in the year AD 35 and established a place where he could bring Mary Magdalene and her son Jesus. The following year, this is what occurred and Mary (now pregnant again), son Jesus and John (Joseph of Arimathea) moved to Southern France.

They landed at Marseilles but moved fairly quickly to the region around the Pyrenees and eventually to Carcassonne. Mary Magdalene became a part of the local Jewish community and continued her life much as she had lived it within the community at Qumran and John took to spreading the teachings of the Tables of Testimony as interpreted by Jesus the Christ. Jesus, after several years of journeying and teaching also came to Carcassonne and fathered a second daughter.

The Templar Energy Grid

In his capacity as teacher and protector John, with his nephew Jesus, arrived in Glastonbury in 56 AD and it is at this point that Merlin rejoins the story.

Merlin's primary role is to protect and assist the planet in its support of human and animal life. The role is primarily one of providing new, and balancing old, energies. In his task as ambassador for the teachings of the true form and purpose of mankind, John required a new energy basis for the dissemination of this information, an extension of the energy links into the Temple of Solomon and the network already established for the Brotherhood of Sion. A new network was begun by Merlin which worked alongside and parallel to the energy matrix already linking Silbury, Glastonbury and Stonehenge with the other energy sites within Britain and Europe. It is this new network which was to form the later Templar grid.

With this new energy intact, John began the process of teaching the old knowledge around the West of Britain and established a teaching centre at Glastonbury. This teaching centre has been assumed to be the first Christian church established anywhere outside of Rome but it was really more of a synagogue than a Christian establishment. The name 'Britain' is derived from the Welsh Celtic word B'rith - ain meaning 'Covenant Land'.

With the teaching centre established, the Brotherhood of Sion began to actively recruit members in Britain and by AD 70 there were a growing number of travelling teachers. It is this movement which began the Celtic Church and reawakened the majority of the people in Britain.

Britain was, and still is, the primary energy exchange on the planet. Those who lived in Britain had the easiest access to this energy and this is why it was possible for them to "wake up" fairly quickly. Whilst there are many energy points on the planet, all linking into the British primary source, the energy remains at its most powerful in Britain.

With the work begun in Britain, John returned to France taking Jesus (the son) with him and began his teaching there. To assist in this task, Merlin extended the energy linkages through France to Carcassonne.

Whilst all of this was taking place, the Romans sacked Jerusalem in AD 70 and the tribes of Israel were scattered. Qumran was also eventually overrun and the teachings were suspended. The "time vault" under the temple was not discovered and so the Ark of the Covenant and the treasure buried with it remained intact. Many of those displaced from Jerusalem and Qumran travelled to France and established a new community which lived within the new teachings. The people who belonged to this community eventually became known as the Cathars.

Also around this time Jesus' three children married into local families and three new branches of the Davidic line were begun and the dynasty of the Morovingian kings became established.

Merlin, during this time, monitored the progress of those in Britain and France to establish whether the Sion plan had any chance of success. New energy grids were established and Britain, France, Germany, Russia and Palestine were all linked together within the new energy grid. The beginnings of a coherent return to humanity's full consciousness. With this work complete, Merlin leaves the human realms to humanity to continue their reawakening and in AD 145 he travels to Avalon to work with the Sidhé.

Disinformation and Persecution

In the meantime, The Church of Rome (Christian) had begun to form and many factions were present from the very beginning. The teachings of the church eventually took on the form of the teachings of Paul and a whole new version of events and doctrines began mainly based around the concept of Jesus as a divine being. Needless to say they had nothing whatsoever to do with the actual teachings of Jesus the Christ.

Within this period there were two forms of Christian beliefs being taught; there was the Pauline version which was eventually adopted by the Roman Church and there were the actual teachings of Jesus. The true teachings were suppressed as they presented a threat to the divinity and authority of the Roman Emperors and the followers of Jesus were persecuted and murdered.

The teachings presented by Jesus taught of a state where all people were equal, all faiths tolerated and all were able to regain their true selves. This approach was seen as dangerous by Rome and the story of the persecution and execution of early Christians belong to the Jesus Christians as opposed to the Pauline Christians. It was Rome that eventually prevailed and the "official" version of events presented as a true history of Jesus.

As Roman Christianity became the official church of Rome it began to exert its authority and tried to totally dominate the lands once ruled by the Roman Empire. However, there was huge resistance from those countries who had heard the true teachings and many wars were fought over many centuries. Rome could not do much about the Islamic world but it could attempt to overthrow all opposition within the "Christian" world.

The church made huge advances, mainly by putting opposition to the sword and by about 480 AD began to make advances into the regions who followed the true teachings. At this time Merlin returned to observe the human world and, with extreme reluctance, removed the Sidhé from the realm of men in the year 538 to save them from the advancing hordes of the church. If the Sidhé had remained within the human realm, they would have been destroyed by the church as they were a part of the knowledge of Atlantis and the church would not tolerate full knowledge of their existence as they were the creationary aspect of the planet. How could a church that taught that their god was The Creator of all life deal with full human knowledge that the planet played a major role in the creation of many elements of life on Earth except by attempting the full destruction of the Sidhé?

The Brotherhood of Sion attempted many times to stop this destruction of the truth and in some regions they were successful. However, with the Catholic Church taking to itself the role of appointing kings, many of the old kingdoms were overrun and puppet rulers installed.

Against this climate and to minimise the potential problems of having removed the Sidhé, in 540 Merlin took on a full adult physical body and began a life that was to span 900 years (see previous chapter).

The Ark of the Covenant

For many years Merlin travelled widely looking, listening and talking to as many people as possible to find out what their beliefs were and how they saw the threat of the Church of Rome. Everywhere he found a need for change as many people were aware of the energy changes but could not place the need for change into any recognisable context and it was this confusion that the church was capitalising on. By persuading people that they were the new force for change and good, they won many converts and once they were converted, there was very little chance of leaving.

Against this background, there was little that Merlin could do other than to return to Britain and France and enhance and reinforce the new energy grids established to bring about the change begun by the Brotherhood of Sion.

By 790 the first stages of an enhanced grid had been established linking Britain, Scotland and France and a new plan formulated between Merlin and the Brotherhood of Sion.

This plan involved the bringing of the Ark of the Covenant out of Jerusalem and back to France. All that was required to bring this plan to fruition was a suitable opportunity.

Since the end of the Roman Empire, Jerusalem had been controlled by Islamic forces who saw the taking of the city as a great triumph against Rome and the Roman Church. Given the Church saw Islam as its greatest enemy, they were particularly incensed by this occupation of the region they saw as the seat of their religion. The Church was also searching for the Ark of the Covenant as a means of obtaining credibility and control over many other religious groups. The church knew that the Ark was in Jerusalem but did not know where or how to unlock the time vault.

To counter this threat to their lands and their beliefs, in 876 the Brotherhood of Sion established an organisation which was apparently Christian but with the express purpose of returning the Ark to the Brotherhood. Their secondary role was to act as armed protectors against the threat of the Church. These were the Knights Templar.

Most history books will put the establishment of the Knights Templar somewhere between 1040 and 1080 this is because it is around this time that they became public and were active in the first Crusade but the need for protection from the Catholic Church had begun much earlier and the Knights' initial role was one of armed protection with their actual purpose to be fulfilled when an opportunity arose.

In 1095 Jerusalem was overrun by the Moslems and many in Europe saw this as a loss of their Holy Land. An attempt to retake Jerusalem by many thousands of ordinary people (The Peasants Crusade) had failed and the Roman Church called for a Holy Crusade to regain Palestine but particularly Jerusalem. Although the Crusades were seen as a "Holy War" between Christians and the Moslems, the real purpose was the Church of Rome attempting to remove the Ark from its place of safe keeping. Whoever controlled the energy and knowledge of the Ark could take control, if the knowledge contained within it was used to control others, of all humanity and this was the motive of the Roman Church.

Under the disguise of the Crusade, a French Duke, Godefroi de Bouillon, led the Knights Templar in the first Crusade of 1099 and was successful in taking Jerusalem where he was installed as the "King". With the Templars gaining safe access to the temple site, Merlin arrived and removed the time lock. Merlin then established an energy link (gateway) between Jerusalem and the Cistercian monastery in Clairvaux in France, the 'headquarters' of the Brotherhood of Sion, and the Ark and other treasures were transported through the gate.

The End of the Templars

The treasure of Solomon amounted to a vast sum of money sufficient for the Knights to become the most powerful and influential money lenders in Europe. However, the greatest treasure of all was the contents of The Ark of the Covenant, The Tables of Testimony.

These 'Tables' were the records of Atlantis and other knowledge which had the potential to change the world as it existed at that time. Again, it was Merlin who helped to unlock its secrets. The 'Tables' were recorded within a green crystal and knowledge of how to read the information had been forgotten. Merlin was able to construct an energy matrix which allowed the contents to be read, translated and understood by the Brotherhood and the Knights.

The first signs of the wealth and the new knowledge was the beginnings of the construction of the Notre Dame Cathedrals throughout France. These buildings were spectacular in their form and their construction. All tall buildings, up until this time, relied on massive wall constructions, the taller the building, the thicker the walls. With this knew knowledge, wall thickness could be greatly reduced and buildings given the appearance of light and grace. To further work with this kind of knowledge a new branch of the Knights Templar was formed and became known as The Freemasons.

The Knights Templar set about disseminating this knowledge as freely as they could. The Cathars were a natural outlet for this information as were all of the lands ruled by the Morovingian Kings who welcomed the enlightening of their peoples.

The Roman Church was totally opposed to this process. They had built their empire on fear and withholding information, having someone come along and show that they had deliberately employed this method to subjugate the masses was totally unacceptable and conflict began to arise.

The Templars also began to lend money on a vast scale, either to causes they considered worthy or, secretly, to those who were against the Templar cause. By lending money to their enemies, the Templars began to exert control and bring their knowledge to a greater public. One such person was King Philippe IV of France who owed the Templars a great deal of money and was extremely afraid of their power. He persuaded the Pope, Clement V to support his persecution and a Papal decree was issued leading to the destruction of the Templars in France and England.

On Friday the 13th of October 1307 (the origin of the expression that Friday the 13th is unlucky for some), the French King ordered that all Templars be killed and their lands and goods taken into the care of the crown. Fortunately, some of the Templars heard of the plan just in time and the Ark of the Covenant was safely taken out of France and away from the Pope.

This action effectively destroyed the Templars in France and they moved their seat of governing to Scotland where the Ark is still kept in a time vault similar to the one constructed by Solomon under his temple.

The Brothers of Sion also now reinforced their positions in Germany, Scotland, Russia and Palestine. The remainder of Sion records were given to the Cathars for safe keeping in Carcassone.

Merlin assisted the Brotherhood to extend their energy grid into these regions and the Brotherhood and the Templars went to ground to await a more auspicious time when they could once again help mankind to reawaken.

In 1340, with this phase of the work completed and the Ark safe, Merlin removed himself from his physical body and returned to Macchu Picchu to rest and contemplate.

Author's Note

The Akashic contains all that has happened on Earth. However, it is not always possible to obtain clear information about specific dates. In this chapter, I have drawn heavily on the book Bloodline Of The Holy Grail by Lawrence Gardner for some specifics and details.

This does not mean that the Akashic fully tallies with Lawrence Gardner's book, just that some of the detail he provides is very accurate and fits into the narrative of this book very well.

Chapter Ten

Completions

The Human Plan has an end. At the beginning of The Plan, an absolute time limit for completion was set for the end of the year 2011. This was a collective choice. The planet, the Thirteen and all of the races involved with The Human Plan all agreed on this completion date. The reasons for this are quite complex but essentially come down to the energies available for humanity to fulfil its chosen task are coming from outside of our solar system. They are routed through the gateway of Orion and into the thirteen primary energy centres on the planet's surface. These energies come to a halt in 2011. This was the plan and there appears to be no alternative but to complete before that date.

Every single individual who has been involved, directly or indirectly, in The Plan is fully aware of this date of completion. The only recorded version of the time frame that still remains is the Mayan Calendar.

What this calendar records is the various stages and intentions of the time frame for change and development that The Plan envisaged. All of the potential times that change could have occurred are recorded on the stones of the calendar. As far as humanity is concerned, the world does end in 2011 as if we fail to complete our chosen task, Earth will no longer be available to us.

This is why Merlin felt that finding the source of the new energies was of paramount importance. Unless the reasons for the disruptions to human development could be found, mankind could no longer remain on this world.

As we approached the end of the nineteenth century, our time for completion was running short. Of all of the many attempts to bring humanity to its senses that had taken place throughout history, none had succeeded. Merlin had instigated a change of energies on the planet at the beginning of the 1800s to try and provide a new impetus for change. These energies began to make people realise that they had accepted dominance by others and began to bring the problems to the surface. The armed revolts in India, China, Spain, Africa etc. were all brought about by people attempting to take back their own power and responsibilities, spurred on by these new frequencies.

All of these mini wars led to shaking the foundations of the empires then in place, rocking them so much that it culminated in the First World War.

It is called the 'war to end all wars' for two reasons. The first was that it did actually have that effect. All of the various armed struggles taking place globally came to an end and by 1919 the world was at peace. The second reason is that it was intended to sweep away all of the past. It should have been sufficient to alter the direction of humanity, free it from its imperialist past and move it into change ahead of the 2011 deadline.

It nearly succeeded.

The world and all of humanity changed but it did not change enough. Many of the old values and controls remained in place. Many were reluctant to let go of their positions of power and were sufficient to halt the new direction. Many souls left in despair. With the realisation that change was not about to begin, a flu epidemic swept the world and more died from the flu than had during the five years of war. The impetus for change had once again been halted by these strange energies. Not all was lost however.

Many of those who remained physical began to change society. A newer, freer openness filtered through all levels of life. Many began to 'wake up' to the realities of who they are and began to explore levels of consciousness which, up until then, had remained unknown. Areas of new exploration of the planet also began and some of the ancient societies, especially Egypt, were rediscovered with wonder.

Many books were written about past lives and channelling works were, for the first time, readily available and read widely. The memories of Atlantis were reawakened in many and, for a time, it looked as though change might just be possible.

But again, as so many times in the past, change was blocked and physical materialism once again took hold. This time though it could not be fully sustained. There was sufficient impetus from those who had begun to awaken to slow down the quest for power and wealth and the great depression of the 1930's resulted.

Once again, the industrialists and bankers took over and brought humanity back into their powerful clutches.

Time was rapidly running out, there were only seventy years left to complete The Plan. Fifteen thousand years of human problems only had seventy years to be resolved. Seventy years left to put all of the accumulated knowledge, Karma, to use. Into this situation stepped a very brave soul. This was someone who was prepared to take the hate of humanity and reflect it back. Someone who was to act as a mirror to show the world the depths of depravity it was prepared to go before we collectively said stop. History records his physical name as Adolf Hitler.

Following the First World War, many checks and balances were put into place to prevent Germany once again starting a world war. At the start of his political career, Hitler began to push the limits of The Treaty of Versailles to see if anyone said stop. Despite having every warning from Hitler, the world governments allowed him to continue. He was, after all, the same as them. The leader of a country who was seemingly attempting to rebuild the economy and industry following the War and the depression. He should be encouraged and given a large degree of latitude even when Hitler began to build up his armed forces. He was very enterprising, had many new ideas and showed how it was possible to fool the population, through education and propaganda, that they were the master race. Under the disguise of 'purifying' the German peoples, he developed Eugenics which appealed to many industrialists and world leaders. New ways of controlling the masses were brought about and found support in many areas of society. Here was a man who was brave enough to act and many applauded him.

It was only when Hitler did what he said he was going to do and invaded Poland that someone said stop and the world once again went to war.

Following the war, the world had actually changed. It had achieved what the First World War had not, it freed people from the hold of the past and brought a new equality to society. Some tried to reimpose the old but were stopped. Humanity was finally beginning to turn.

By the middle of the 1950's, however, the industrialists were growing in strength. Companies who were looking for world markets were beginning to rise and forcing the beginning of a global economy. All of the war industrial capacity was turned to making goods for the consumer market and the planet was progressively and ruthlessly stripped of its resources. Prior to the Second World War very few man made chemicals existed. Following the war, markets had to be found where the chemical companies could offload their war surpluses and the planet and humanity began to be poisoned.

Only fifty years left to complete the Human Plan.

Seeds of Completion, Seeds of Destruction

As with the aftermath of WW1, many people did wake up to change and the start of the 1960's led to the 'Flower Power' revolution. The 'Hippies' changed the mass consciousness and the world and human attitudes changed with it.

All of society was changed in some way. Nobody escaped from the revolution in thinking and attitudes. Once again, it looked as though it might be possible to bring about some lasting change. And the change did last or at least it sowed the seeds of permanent change.

The industrialists and their strange energy frequencies fought back, of course, and we went through the period at the end of the 1970's and 1980's where once again we had global monetarist policies forcing people back to a work orientated world. Transnational companies sprang up whose annual turnover is greater than the GNP of some countries. Freedoms were eroded at a governmental level because of these companies and political thought now reflected company and not country policy. The people had lost what control they had fought a long hard fight to win. Trade unions' power to act on behalf of their members was quashed and commercialism won. The will of the people for change was being inexorably crushed and the power of the company became all.

With it has come the greatest threat to the completion of The Plan and also the greatest threat to all life on the planet: genetically modified food.

GM is Atlantis revisited. The full cycle of events has come back to haunt us. On Atlantis we were considerably further up the consciousness scale than we are now and the only way we could control our mistakes then was to destroy a continent. Now, the planet is once again at risk of destruction and this time, there is no one who can help us. The Sidhé cannot be brought back whilst humanity is still in the throes of change as their existence is in danger from the human world yet only the Sidhé have the capability of stopping the menace of GM.

Final Choices

With the end of the 1980's came the realisation that we only had twenty years left to complete The Plan.

Merlin was no closer to finding out where the strange range of energy frequencies that had caused so much disruption throughout human history had come from. But those who had most access to these strange energies acted and attempted to prevent Merlin from seeing The Plan through.

A way was found to limit the actions that Merlin could take to either find the source of these energies or to act against them in his full capacity. The block was very effective and it took Merlin six years before he could undo the block sufficiently to set the next course of events into action.

Built into The Plan were a sequence of events that would begin as The Plan approached its completion. If humanity had not changed by 1995, sixteen years before the end of The Plan, these sequences would come into play.

Merlin's role is to be the guardian of the planet and to assist humanity to its chosen completion. If humanity had not played its part fully and time had run out, humanity has to leave the planet. With the ending of 1995, energies within the mass consciousness were triggered and set into motion a sequence of events which we are currently working through. Regardless of the block put onto Merlin, these events have begun to be played out.

The first is that in August 1996 everyone on the planet was asked, by the mass consciousness, to assess their own state of readiness to complete The Plan. This question was asked on a higher self level to ensure an honest answer.

The reply was that a total of forty percent of the population felt able and willing to complete their chosen tasks. Although this sounds like a low percentage it actually represents many millions of people. As far as The Plan is concerned, if only one person completed, The Plan would be a success.

It also means that sixty percent of the total population stated that they could not complete the plan. In other words, these individuals decided by themselves on their own assessment of the work they had completed, they could not accommodate their total consciousness within their physical bodies. Since their decision, these individuals have been leaving the planet. It is important to stress at this point that everyone on Earth has arrived here from somewhere other and have lived many lifetimes taking part in The Human Plan. It was their decision to come here and their decision to take part. Nobody stood in judgement of these souls. Each and every one of those who are leaving are leaving because they chose to do so. Those who are staying have also chosen to do so, nobody judged them either.

All who are connected with Earth at this time have been fully aware of this choice ever since they arrived. It is and always has been an intrinsic part of The Plan if we ever arrived at this point where The Plan had not been completed and we were running out of time. It was a fail-safe mechanism to ensure that those who had completed their part of the process were not removed from the planet when the time ran out.

Those who have completed their work are undergoing their own integration process in their own way. Those who decided that they were unready are leaving the planet to return to their 'home' realms without any recriminations or penalties. This is the universe of free choice and all have freely chosen. Nobody has had their free choice removed from them in the making of their decision.

New Energies

As for Merlin, he was having difficulties. In his attempt to discover the source of the strange energies that had altered the natural course of The Plan, he had discovered that a specific group of individuals was involved. These individuals had taken on a set of energy frequencies which allowed them to act in a way which could remove the free choice of others. This group seems to have an interest in preventing The Plan from completing. The ultimate course of their actions is that all life on Earth is destroyed.

This group had somehow found a way of effectively binding and blinding him, limiting the actions that Merlin could take. It took several years before Merlin could partially break through this binding and progress with his part of the completion of The Plan.

With the ending of WW1 and the partial awakening of a number of people, several groups have been at work on the planet undoing much of the harm that humanity has done. These individuals have usually acted alone or in small groups with no knowledge of the work they were doing. Collectively these small groups and individuals have been paving the way for the connection of new energies to the earth in order for The Plan to be completed. Merlin's part in this was to make the final connection of these energies.

Since the 1930's the old lay line grid has been cleansed and a new 'clean' lay line network constructed that weaves in with and supersedes the old lay grid. Built into this new grid are thirteen primary energy centres one of which being the new energy intake point. At 6.00 pm BST on the 14th of August 1996, Merlin made the final connections of the new energy feed. This connection, through Orion, powered up the other twelve primary energy points world-wide and activated the new lay grid. This new energy intake incorporates 6 000 000 dimensions of energy and is effectively limitless. This new grid provides the energies to complete the human integration process and allows the planet to draw on this energy for its needs as it progresses through a change of its own (see appendix one).

The connection of these energies also released a low frequency pulse around the planet which resonates with our DNA. DNA is our primary memory system where all of our existences as physical beings are remembered. What this pulse was designed to do was to release any unwanted memories from our past to allow room to take on more of the total consciousness.

The final aspects of The Plan were beginning and nothing could stop it. Each individual who had decided to complete the process now had the energies available to power the change. Those who had decided to leave also had the power to complete their part of the journey and travel home.

The Final Answer

By finally releasing himself from the bindings designed to stop this whole process it was possible for Merlin, with a lot of help from a Pleiadean friend, to track down the source of the energies that had caused so much interference throughout human history.

In order for a universe to exist, it is brought into being by a thought generated in 'the fields of possibility' we call The Creator. Our universe explores the thought of absolute freedom of choice. Other universes exist that explore other thoughts. A universe has a lifetime, a span of time in which it explores its particular thought, and then the energies contained within the thought return to source, in other words the universe collapses, and the knowledge gained from the exploration of the thought enhances the knowledge of the fields of possibility.

One such collapse occurred to a universe relatively close to ours and one group of the inhabitants of that universe attempted to escape through what astronomers would call a 'worm hole'. This is where a black hole makes contact with another black hole and the theoretical travel of energies is in both directions.

The worm hole was connected to a region of our universe which does not contain any life and so remained undetected until very recently. The energy flow from the other universe was too small to detect, especially when it first opened and so was not noticed for some time. The worm hole event occurred three and a half million years ago.

The Solar System is unique. In order to bring about the levels of life that were intended, several unusual features were put into place. The main difference between this solar system and all others was the inclusion of 'guardians' to each of the original thirteen planets. When the first two consciousnesses, that were the constructors of the two planets who left the 'experiment', pulled out of the experiment, not only did their actions create massive destruction within the solar system, their action also ripped away part of the consciousnesses that were their guardians.

It must be understood that nobody could predict the consequences of the first two planets leaving. The uniqueness of the solar system meant that actions such as these had repercussions which had never been experienced before at any point in the history of the universe. By suddenly leaving the planetary structures that these consciousnesses had constructed around themselves, the aspect of their guardian that had 'linked' into the planet was also ripped away. This meant that these two guardians were dramatically affected.

The two guardians whole purpose of existence was to work with these planets and their destruction, without any kind of warning, left them confused, disorientated and 'homeless'. In their confused state, they left the solar system and eventually encountered the wormhole connected to the other universe.

Their whole purpose of being was to encourage and nurture new life. By discovering the new life from the other universe, in their confused state, they began to encourage those who would enter this universe from another. In doing so, they unleashed energies so incompatible with this universe that it nearly caused its destruction.

This universe has an energy construction that allows for the total freedom of choice for each individual to choose to take any actions they wish as long as it does not remove the free choice of others to act. The energies introduced from the other universe allowed those who came into contact with them to act in ways which could remove the free choice of others. In addition to this, those who came from the other universe were in search of resources and they began to strip this universe of everything they could find. Those who came from this other universe have become known, within the Akashic, as 'The Fourteenth Faction'.

Every attempt had been made to protect the Earth's abundant life but around 395 BC, 33 000 individuals, from The Six, on their way to Earth became contaminated by these very peculiar frequencies. It is still unclear whether they took these new energies on deliberately or were just caught in the blast. Either way, it meant that they had taken on energies that were not compatible with this universe and gave them the capability of removing the free choice of others. Making use of these energies, however, was still a matter of free choice. If they had so chosen, they could have thrown off these frequencies and asked The Thirteen to take care of the matter and restore the correct energy balance. They did not and two and a half thousand years of problems resulted.

This was the source of the problems Merlin had been attempting to track. This was why the Human Plan had been disrupted and this was why humanity had begun to destroy each other and strip the planet of its resources. At last, the answer.

With these individuals active on Earth, the energies of The Human Plan became twisted and many people became influenced by those who made use of these energies.

Once the worm hole was discovered, it took a number of people working together for some time to close the rift. The energies from the other universe have been disposed of by the Thirteen of this universe.

These energies no longer exist on this universe and especially not on Earth. Those who wielded these energies for their personal gain no longer have access to these energies and their influence is rapidly diminishing.

Other Problems

There has also been an influence on human thought and action in the past sixty years but this has been more specialised in its influence.

There are a group within this universe who those who have an interest in UFO's call 'The Greys'. The greys are a species who have had an interest in the earth for many thousands of years. They use energy as their primary source of food, particularly emotional energy. They have visited earth many times over the aeons particularly at times of strife where they have gathered the energies generated by fear and used them as a source of food. This does not mean that they have taken individuals and extracted fear from them but, for want of a better description, 'surfed' the mass consciousness and made use of the energetic aspect of fear within the mass consciousness as a food source.

With the crash at Roswell in the 1950's, contact was made between the American military and the greys and a partnership, of sorts, has been in place ever since. The Akashic is quite clear about this.

Since entering into the partnership the American military have allowed the greys greater access to the planet than they have previously had and virtually all of the animal and human abductions have been carried out by this species with the blessing of the American military. In return, the American military have gained major technological information about space flight and stealth technology.

Given that humanity has been influenced by the fourteenth faction, industrialists, banks, religions and many other sources, fear is a common emotion on this planet. With good access granted by the American military, many greys have entered into our solar system and made free use of our emotional overload. They have done this in ways which have generally not been noticed and have taken on various disguises to hide their presence.

Some greys also took on the fourteenth energy and have been using these altered energies to influence the actions of some on Earth, particularly within the military and secret services. These combined influences, grey and military, have usually taken the form of psychic attacks on individuals, groups and the mass consciousness in order to engender a strong emotional response on a planet wide scale.

Their most common disguise used by the greys themselves is to contact either individuals or groups of people in the name of being 'Ascended Masters' and frequently adopt the name of a religious leader from human history, Saint Germaine being a popular one.

Within the Akashic, there is no record of 'Ascended Masters' before the Roswell crash and the title is meaningless within any context. Their influence has spread far and wide mainly because of human ego. If someone is channelling an 'Ascended Master' then the channeller must be someone 'special'. These channellers then attract around them those who are easily influenced by their egos and the grey masquerading as an 'Ascended Master' has a readily available source of 'food'.

The grey access to our solar system is through a gateway located in the southern hemisphere constellation of Draco which has been shut to them since September 2000. All greys remaining within the sphere of Earth have been rounded up by Merlin and many others and evicted from our solar system.

The Legacy of Atlantis
Another region of problems and abductions is a left over legacy from Atlantis.

We have touched upon some of the problems encountered towards the end of Atlantis where a number of souls were placed in a position of severe torture. Some self inflicted, some imposed by experimentation with animal genetic structures. The reality of the torment and horror caused by these experiments cannot be conveyed in words.

How can you convey the horrors felt by so many of these 'people' when we do not have the vocabulary to describe the physical forms they constructed and then tried to come to terms with.

Many cultures, especially Indian, Tibetan and Sumerian describe monstrous animals and human hybrids who inhabit deep caves who appear randomly and abduct animals and people, especially women and children, and then disappear. These are descriptions of the actions and appearances of those souls who could not face humanity and could not live above ground.

The beginnings of the experiments had come about because of the wish to honour the animal group that an individual worked with. In taking responsibility for the particular animal's 'etheric' template, the individuals involved began to delve deeply into the ways of the animals and slowly immersed themselves in the animal mass consciousness. As they became more deeply connected in this way, they felt that it would be appropriate to show their connection by adopting some aspects of that particular animal's physical appearance into their own.

The initial adaptation process was usually one where the person altered their genetic structures sufficiently to have the skin of the animal instead of their own. Once this process was begun, many others on Atlantis saw the alteration of human skin to animal skin as attractive and a 'fashion' began where all sorts of skin types were chosen.

Most of those who took on skins for reasons of fashion were largely unaffected by their transitions and remained totally human. However, those who took on the characteristics and worked within the animal's mass consciousness, began to change their behaviour.

It should be remembered that at this period of human history, those who came to Atlantis were a full consciousness within the physical body. It is difficult for us, at this time, to comprehend the full meaning of this. We are so used to having our total consciousness 'divided' into two, the physical aspects and the 'higher self' division, that the capabilities of a fully integrated consciousness are largely beyond our understanding.

The total consciousness spans a massive range of energy frequencies. This combination of frequencies allows us to communicate freely with all forms of life from the simplest bacteria to the consciousness that is a galaxy. All communications take place on a psychic level. That is, there is free movement of thought patterns which can incorporate all of the information we are choosing to communicate. Pictures, sounds, smells, impressions and many other types of information can be communicated in this way without the use of language or gesture. It allows us to psychically delve as deeply as we wish into the structures of the world around us. Plants trees, water, air or any other organism can be investigated and communicated with to any degree.

This level of communication is what we had come to know and expect on Atlantis and communication with animals was especially enjoyed. Into this open and free level of trust another factor was introduced. If the person communicated with their chosen animal on these very deep levels and then added some the animal's genetic structures to their own, that person started to take on other characteristics of that animal. Communicating with animals was not a problem. Altering gene sequences to take on animal skin was not a problem. But, the combination of the two acts did begin to cause problems. It was a slow process but one which had many far reaching and deeply acting consequences.

Say, for example, someone chose to work with the mass consciousness of a herbivore, such as a cow. Taking on their skin whilst working within the etheric template meant that you began to develop a growing interest in grass. Carnivorous animals hunt to survive and taking on the genetic structures of such animals whilst working within their etheric template meant you began to take an interest in hunting and your natural prey becomes a human.

Put together with the slowing of the higher brain functions by the planet's natural energy structures and we ended up with a human predator who took other humans, sometimes as food but mainly for further experimentation on the influences of animal genetics on the human form.

In addition, many others did not work with animals but on themselves. Could the body's form or function be enhanced or altered in different ways? Whilst we did not reproduce sexually at this time, as most chose to be androgynous, could we nevertheless take on sexual organs of either sex and enhance them to make them larger or to function in different ways. Was sexual reproduction possible by humans? At this time no one knew but there was a great curiosity to find out. For example, once a full reproductive system was developed, it would be easier to find out the various stages of foetus development if the body could be modified so that the uterus was external to the body.

Did the size of the body matter? Could bone and muscle structures be modified to enhance them to their physical limits, at both ends of the scale? Would there be any advantages to one arm being more highly muscular than the other? Would enhancing the legs for running at extreme speeds be useful? If breasts had multiple nipples could a number of children be fed at the same time?

The possibilities were all explored and as we began to lose the higher brain functions, these experiments became more and more bizarre until, ultimately, the two regions of experimentation were mixed together. Human and animal experimentation were worked on together and the worst possible scenario arose.

Several miles beneath the Earth's surface is a strata known as the Mohorovicic Layer. This is where the core's magma flows around the globe and vents from this layer give rise to volcanoes. When the volcanoes are spent, or the magma pressure released, the magma flow cools leaving huge caverns and a network of tunnels. To escape the wrath of the Atlanteans and to avoid the purging of the experiments and experimenters that took place towards the end of Atlantis, many of the worst examples of these genetic experiments hid themselves away in the deep cave systems that link in to this deep layer.

Many have chosen to continue their experiments whilst living in these layers and have been joined by some of those of 'grey' origin. From these depths, these beings have risen to the surface and carried out many abductions over thousands of years. The stories of strange creatures suddenly appearing and removing people or animals from the surface and disappearing back into caves are these experimenters looking for new raw material or food.

The last recorded account of such raids took place in Puerto Rico in 1995. Eye witness accounts also came from Mexico, Southern Florida and the desert regions of south west America at the same time.

155

All of these 'catacomb' regions have now been cleared of these life form experiments and the souls involved have been helped by the universal races to rehabilitate them back into universal life.

As of May 2002, Earth is finally clear of outside influence and The Human Plan can be brought to its conclusion.

Biotechnology

There is one thing to note, however, and that is the problem of genetically modified organisms.

There are two regions of responsibility for the life on Earth. Animals are the responsibility of humanity. Plants are the responsibility of the Sidhé and the faerie. Whilst humanity can 'play' with plant material, when mistakes occur, it is only the Sidhé who have the capability of undoing those mistakes. Humanity does not have the abilities necessary to correct the mistakes they make with these organisms.

The way in which GM plants are produced is not generally known. In order to transfer the chosen gene sequence into a plant, a transfer organism called a 'vector' is used. Vectors are bacteria or viruses which the scientists have implanted with a gene sequence from another form of life and use the vector to transfer that gene sequence into the target seeds. The most commonly used vector is a bacteria called E-Coli 147, the one that causes food poisoning.

In their search for more efficient forms of transfer, and greater profits to the GM company, scientists have developed new forms of vectors by genetically modifying the bacteria themselves. This form of genetic modification allows the bacteria to be powerful enough to cross any species barrier. What this means in reality is that if you take your dog for a walk in a field of GM crop containing these particular vectors, you, your dog and the plant start swapping genes. The result of that process, or any other contact with these vectors and any other organism, is that we have complete genetic meltdown. In other words, by the time we should have finished The Human Plan, 2011, if these vectors are let loose, there will not be any life left on the planet for us to communicate with.

These vectors have the power and the capability of mixing genes with all species. In a very short period of time we have a genetic soup where no form of life is recognisable and all life ceases.

Neither humans, the NGC, Pleiadeans nor Merlin have the capability of undoing this damage. Only the Sidhé have that capability. The Sidhé have refused to return to the surface of the planet until humanity has made its change. The race is on.

Energies have been put in place by Merlin that accelerate the change process. The 2011 completion date for The Human Plan has been brought forwards because of this threat. Those who are undergoing the consciousness integration process must complete their work by the end of 2005 by the absolute latest or the paradise that is Earth will be lost to the universe. All life on Earth will cease and the unbelievable abundance of life that the Earth has created will no longer exist. The threat is this immediate and this serious.

The only thing that can now stop humanity achieving its goal is GM.

Chapter Eleven

Future Roles

The discovery of the 'Fourteenth Faction' has explained a great deal about human history. It has also freed Merlin to return to his original role, that of providing energies for the planet and all of its life.

The first act Merlin has undertaken has been to cleanse the mass consciousness of the fear generated by the Fourteen energies.

The use made of the ability to remove the free choice of others has engendered a great deal of fear within the population as a whole. Underlying all such acts of removal of choice is the sense that there has been a shift in the way in which humanity has been able to function. This underlying unease has manifested itself as a sense of not knowing how to respond to the individuals who took to themselves these unnatural energies. Subconsciously, humanity has recognised the fact that "something" was wrong but, like Merlin, could not understand the reasons for the change in direction. It is this not knowing that has created a layer of fear within the mass consciousness.

This layer of fear has allowed those who would take control of others to manipulate the masses in ways which held the fear in place and a fearful population is one which is easily controlled.

This has been a pattern throughout the last two and a half thousand years of human history. One individual imposes their will upon another and a cycle of events follow which create despondency and fear. Control is then exerted by implying that the fear can be released by supporting the policies of those who would control. As humanity has fallen into this trap, further control has been applied and we have a population which has difficulty seeing that the control exists and steering a way out of the situation becomes increasingly obscure.

Fortunately, not all people fell into the clutches of these energies and there was always a section of the population who fought against the complete control of those who would master humanity.

The peculiarity of these Fourteen energies cannot be stressed strongly enough. The whole purpose of the thought behind this universe is to explore the possibilities offered where absolute free choice exists. Part of the choice made by those who inhabit this universe was to experiment with full physical existence as experienced on Earth.

In forming the physical worlds an abundance of life sprang into being which was entirely unexpected. So much within this solar system provided such a joy of being that a great deal of the resources of this universe were expended upon developing and maintaining it. Into this abundance of life entered a group of beings from another universe whose sole purpose was to obtain resources for themselves and the energies they brought with them allowed for the removal of the primary thought upon which this universe was constructed, namely free choice.

The Fourteenth Faction's aims were to remove as much of the abundance of this universe and draw it back to the remnants of their own universe in order to sustain their refusal to return to the Creationary source. This does not imply that they were exercising free choice as their universe did not allow for that possibility. Their universe explored the thought of control. If every inhabitant of that universe could have control over everyone else, did that bring around a balance where free choice could exist? The answer proved to be a situation where their universe was totally stripped of virtually every resource and the envelope, of that universe, imploded in on itself destroying all life.

A small group had found a way of protecting themselves from the collapse and had searched for a way of entering this universe to strip it of its resources for their own use. There was no thought of the impact their actions would have on the inhabitants of our universe.

The 'management' of this universe, the thirteen beings, were unaware of the activities of the new arrivals from the other universe for some time. Once the problem was identified, their first action was to protect our solar system at all costs. Their actions saved the solar system for some considerable time and at great cost to the resources of the universe. Eventually, those who had taken on board elements of the Fourteen energies broke through the protective barriers and the Earth began to be stripped of its resources although instead of being taken back to the other universe, it became accepted practice for the resources to be converted to money and kept by those who could take control. The prime example of this kind of asset stripping was the industrial revolution.

Since the Earth has become industrialised, humanity has been slowly but surely destroying the planet. At the start of the twenty first century, we have now arrived at the point where the Earth can no longer replenish the natural resources we are stripping on an annual basis. In other words, all that humanity takes from the Earth in one year, in the way of crops (food and trees) and water, the planet takes more

160

than one year to replenish. Other resources, such as coal, oil, gas, metals, etc. cannot be replaced at all.

Fortunately, there have been those who have not accepted the role of these industrialists and scientists and have fought against their actions. In doing so they have raised the awareness of humanity as a whole and there are the beginnings of a revival of human responsibilities and awareness of human actions.

With the switching on of the new primary energy intake in August 1996, humanity began to change and move towards its chosen integration of the consciousness into the physical body. The energies of the Fourteen generated conflict within this process and many faltered. However, these unwelcome energies have now been fully removed from the solar system and the universe and humanity has begun to settle into its chosen task.

The removal of these energies has given massive impetus for change and the signs of acceleration of change to meet our deadline are everywhere. Those who are used to removing the choices of others are losing their way as they begin to realise that humanity is no longer pliable to their manipulations. They are beginning to resort to acts of massive betrayal and destruction to maintain their position of power but the mood of humanity, as a whole, is one where the fear engendered by these acts of violence is short lived and those responsible for such acts are being found out despite attempting to blame others to mask their actions.

If the threat of GM crops can be avoided, there is nothing to stop humanity completing The Human Plan within the chosen time frame.

Merlin's Future

The energies necessary to fuel these 'changes' are being connected by Merlin. There are other, newer, energies required to be in place before the plan can be completed and the construction of these is in hand.

However, the task is not always an easy one. In recent years, there has arisen a group of individuals who state that they have a desire to 'heal the planet'. Whilst, on the face of it, this sounds like a good cause, the reality is totally different. A human being is made up of three components; the physical body, the 'higher self' and the elements of the total soul that are required to run the physical body. At night, most of the physical aspects of the soul leave the body and connect with the higher self to carry out what could be called 'the night job'. The jobs carried out by the soul at night can range from healing people in war zones or caught up in natural disasters, helping the planet to ease its pressure points as it grows in size, to working with members of their soul origin. As this work is carried out by the whole soul, it is done with integrity and understanding of purpose.

When this work is attempted during the conscious day, the work is done without full understanding and, more often than not, the individual attempting to carry out this work is doing so from a point of ego and using it as a method of avoiding their own issues. The comment "I cannot spend any time working on my issues as I am too busy healing the planet" is a common one amongst these groups and individuals.

The reality is that at least 95% of all work carried out during the waking hours by such groups have to be undone by others during 'the night job'.

This diversion of energies away from the completion process both by Merlin and those undertaking the repair work is slowing down the whole completion of the human plan.

Everyone who is physical on the planet at this time is here to carry out work they have undertaken to do before they came here. Most people have a strong sense of being here for a purpose, a job to do. However, it is not possible to fulfil an individual's chosen tasks until such time as we have completed our integration process.

All of us have innate skills which will allow us to carry out the repair work necessary to bring the Earth back to its original pristine condition, to return the Earth to the paradise that it truly is. Unfortunately, if we began to fully use these skills before the rest of humanity was ready, there would be catastrophe.

To understand this, we need to take a look at what would occur to the very first people to complete the integration process. Given the way in which people function these first to 'ascend' would be treated, at the very least, as curiosities, at worst as some kind of 'god like' characters. The military and scientists would either shoot them or experiment on them, or both. Bringing these latent skills to the fore before the time when such abilities can be accepted would only create havoc.

What needs to be completed first is the journey of the individual. Everyone has chosen to walk a path which leads them to the goal of 'enlightenment'. The best, and surest, way of returning Earth to its paradise state is for each and every individual to complete their chosen path. Forget about the stress of trying to heal the planet and encompass who you truly are. That is the true path to heal the self and to heal the planet!

In healing the self, it releases all of the pent up energies that we all contain and allows each individual's light to shine out into the world. It is then that we can be who we truly are - beings of light.

Merlin can supply all of the energies necessary for each individual to 'shine'. He cannot take that journey for you. It is the individual who has the responsibility of making use of those energies to complete their chosen path.

If Merlin is allowed to complete his work, to overcome humanity's lethargy and unwillingness to complete their changes, then the first group of people to complete their individual integration process will do so before the end of 2003.

The energies that allow for completion also will activate a new connection to the realm of the Sidhé. This will allow the Sidhé to return to the planet for the first time in nearly fifteen hundred years. If the Sidhé can return soon, the dangers of GM crops can be overcome and the planet saved. If the Sidhé do not return soon, the planet's life could be lost and the beauty of Earth will be destroyed.

Completing our own journeys brings about change within the self. Change within the self brings about the completion of The Human Plan. The completion of The Human Plan gives us back the paradise we lost.

The Future Present

This all sounds a little doom and gloom. We are at the end of a seven thousand year knowledge gathering process. We are all geared up to put all of our lessons learned into action. At the end of June 2002, the Akashic records that there are ninety eight million people, world wide, ready to make this final step. Ninety eight million people who have taken control of their lives and their actions and brought themselves to a point where completion, the integration of the whole soul into the physical body, can occur. One in fifty people are ready to take their final leap.

The current human population is around about five thousand million people. The nearly one hundred million people, ready to complete, represent only about one half of one percent of the whole population. There are, of course many millions of others who are not far behind. For these people, they only need to hold true to themselves, complete the work already begun, to join the others waiting for the final energies that will allow the last piece of change to occur.

We are all here to be a part of this change. We are all in a position where change is possible. The future has arrived and mankind is set to make it its own.

Appendix One

The Symptoms of Change

The whole purpose of The Human Plan is to understand the constraints of a physical body, how it functions and how to live within it upon a planet of immense density.

Fifteen thousand years ago we began a process of discovery. Seven thousand years ago we began to accumulate knowledge to help us understand our discoveries. This knowledge gathering process we have come to know by a Sanskrit word, 'Karma'. This is all that the word karma means, "knowledge". The means we have used to gain knowledge is to experience. We have experienced all that this world and the human condition has to offer.

This is where the incorrect concept of karma being a 'debt' process arose. By experiencing all of life, all of the potential experiences that life has to offer, we have interacted with many other souls who have also wished for experience. In this interaction, all possibilities have been explored. On some occasions, we have chosen to undergo our experiences with the same souls over several lifetimes, interchanging and switching roles as we underwent the experiences we chose. If one chose to experience a particular event in one lifetime, the others complicit in that wish might also wish to undergo the same experience for themselves in a subsequent lifetime and call upon the original one to 'give back' their experience to them although free choice always remained. If the people involved did not wish to return the 'favour' the one wishing for the experience would find someone else to help them.

In this way, it has appeared as though there are cycles of cause and effect but all there has been is a wish for experience, an opportunity to gain knowledge. As we experience each event, we store the memory of that event in our DNA. In this way, DNA is always changing and how it can influence future lifetimes.

No event occurs by accident. All events occur because we have chosen them to occur.

Traumatic events are a major part of the knowledge gathering experience. How will the body respond? How will the soul respond? All knowledge. Sometimes, however, the chosen experience was more traumatic than we envisaged and the memory of the event can imprint itself into the body we next construct to experience the next life. Or, most commonly, we will choose to undergo a similar experience in a future lifetime in order to better deal with the trauma of the original event and clear it from our store of memories.

Generally, we have enjoyed our lifetimes' experiences. Human life is something which cannot be experienced anywhere else within this universe. Our interaction with the life of the planet and other physical beings has proven to be something of great joy.

Many have chosen to experience lifetimes of joy and not dealt with the memory of the traumas the soul has wished to better deal with. As we approached the beginning of the twentieth century, and the time of ending of The Plan, many have realised that these accumulated memories of trauma needed to be cleared in a very short period of time and for these people, this lifetime has been one of re experiencing these

167

traumas in order to clear them out of the system. For others, this last lifetime has been one of peace and enjoyment as they have cleared traumatic memories in previous lives.

This memory, DNA, clearing process was the reason for a low level pulse of energy being released when Merlin switched on the new energy intake point in 1996. This pulse carried the frequencies necessary to clear these accumulated traumas and release everyone on the planet of their past.

This pulse also worked on a community, country and global level. As these accumulated memories have been released, they have been brought to the attention of the conscious mind and brought up old feelings. The conflicts and turmoils experienced over the world since 1996 have been the symptoms of clearance.

Where these memories have been let go cleanly, there is peaceful release. Where the individual is still hanging onto some of the emotions of the memories, conflicts have arisen, individually or on a country level. Where the conflict is on an individual level, illnesses have arisen which has given rise to the medical profession claiming the arrival of new viruses. Where the trauma has arisen on a community level, wars have been fought. All symptoms of clearance and change.

We have experienced all that life on this planet has to offer. Everybody who is in physical form at the beginning of the twenty first century has experienced all of these possibilities. Male, female, white, coloured, black, Asian, African, Indian, European, homosexual, heterosexual, etc all have been experienced by each and every individual as part of their knowledge gathering journeys. All adding to the accumulated whole of life.

DNA and Multidimensionality

With this clearance come other aspects of change. When we first arrived on Earth, we designed a physical body which contained the whole consciousness. This meant that the body was lighter in density and contained all of the memories of our individual existences. This meant that our DNA was comprised of thirteen spirals. It is a good indicator of how far we have slipped from our original state when it is considered that we have contained only two spirals of DNA for the last seven thousand years.

When we began our knowledge gathering process, 7 000 years ago, we realised that there was potentially not enough time to gather all of the necessary knowledge together.

To 'drive' the body through a human lifetime we actually only need about ten percent of the total soul (consciousness). This means that the remainder of the consciousness, the 'higher self' could divide itself into human sized pieces and live one or more concurrent lifetimes. We generally live a human life with about twenty five percent of the total soul within the body, the remaining seventy five percent making up the higher self. This still leaves the potential for two concurrent lifetimes to be lived by the total soul.

As we divided ourselves up into two or more 'pieces', each piece of the total soul has explored various variations on a particular theme. Each aspect following a series of lifetimes where the chosen theme was explored fully.

As we undergo the process of drawing the whole soul into the physical, we have to accommodate all of the memories contained within our 'multidimensional' journeyings. Each aspect of the soul must be drawn together into the higher self and the accumulated memories brought into the physical structures, into the physical body, of the one who is to be the 'vessel' for the total soul.

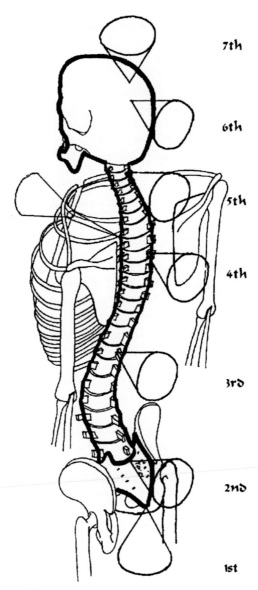

7th

6th

5th

4th

3rd

2nd

1st

The Seven Primary Chakras

As we clear our old memories, we begin to take in the memories of the other aspects of our total selves into our cleansed DNA. As we take on these memories, our DNA begins to grow as these memories are stored away. If the flow of these memories is interrupted, the memory can be brought to the conscious mind and a certain degree of confusion can arise. Many recent cases of so called schizophrenia are an example of this integration process being disrupted.

As we take on board more and more of these memories, our DNA grows and new spirals are added. Many children who have been born in the last decade have up to five DNA spirals already intact making the medical community believe that humanity is mutating into something unknown. We are not mutating, we are integrating.

The Thirteen Chakras of the Soul

Since the start of the karmic cycle, we have had two aspects to the consciousness. The physical aspect which inhabits the physical body and the higher aspect which remains outside of the physical, the higher self. Linking the two aspects together is an energy link which is composed of the higher energy components of the body's chakras. In this way, we have thirteen chakras. Seven located along the spine of the physical body and six within the link to the higher self.

There has always been a degree of confusion about the chakras and their locations. Many have subconsciously recognised that there are thirteen chakras and tried to fit them into the physical body, leading to a great deal of misunderstanding.

The chakras are vortices of energy located along the spine which are aspects of the soul made physical. The energy is then distributed around the body by the meridians. Where the meridians cross, a miniature vortex is formed. It is these miniature vortices that have given rise to the confusion over the location and number of the chakras. In all, there are three hundred and twenty six such crossing points and are used by acupuncturists to clear the energy flow within the meridians. There are only seven chakras within the body.

As we begin our integration, the energies of the six non physical chakras begins to be drawn into the six lower physical chakras. This drawing in alters the energy frequencies within the chakras quite radically.

Traditionally, the chakras have been coloured red, orange, yellow, green, blue, indigo and violet from the first to the seventh. With the integration of the six higher chakras, these colours have changed.

The first becomes a copper gold vortex into which, as it spins, appear 'ribbons' of energy made up of stripes of clear gold, violet and 'petrol' blue. The second chakra becomes a clear 'petrol' blue with ribbons of clear gold, violet and copper gold. The third becomes a clear 'petrol' green with ribbons of clear gold, violet and petrol blue. The fourth chakra changes to a transparent energy shimmer with ribbons of 'flecks' of all of the other colours. The fifth becomes transparent with random flecks of all of the other colours covering the whole surface. The sixth becomes transparent with random flecks of all of the other colours but much fewer than the fifth. The seventh becomes totally transparent without any flecks, just pure energy.

This is the first phase of the integration process, the drawing in of the non physical chakras into the body. With this change, the first chakra takes on an energy frequency higher than the crown chakra used to have. This would appear to be the origin of the practice of 'raising the kundalini'. We have been attempting to raise the energy of the first chakra to that of the crown and there appears to have been a misinterpretation of this process by assuming that you brought the first up to the crown. This brings the lowest energy frequencies of the body up to the highest. The true integration process connects the highest energy to the lowest, thereby raising its energy. Bringing the first up to the crown, raising the kundalini, brought the lowest energy into all of the chakras ultimately causing disruption and confusion. Raising the frequency of the first chakra as high as the crown chakra's frequency brings enlightenment.

Phases of Change

Integrating the energies of the six non physical chakras into the physical chakras is the first phase of the change. Once this is completed all of the colours of the chakras have changed and the DNA has reconstructed seven spirals.

The second phase of the change starts to bring in the energies of the higher self and all of the chakras become totally transparent. As the second phase is undergone, the body's internal organs begin to change and lose most of their density. There is a shell of dense matter but, inside, the organs are pure energy. By the time the second phase is complete, we will have integrated nine spirals to the DNA.

The third phase is where the chakras disappear all together. As the higher self is drawn into the body, it replaces the chakras in turn until the whole of the spine becomes one chakra. In other words, the energies within the spine become one smooth transition of energy frequencies from the lowest at the coccyx to the highest at the crown without there being specific 'points' of energy (chakra locations). As this happens, the bone, muscles and skin become much less dense and we take on an inner 'glow' of energy. At the end of the third phase, we will have integrated eleven spirals to the DNA.

It is unlikely that those who have lived through the integration process will be able to achieve thirteen DNA spirals, that situation will only be possible for those born after we have completed our processes, but at least our work will have cleared the way for those who are to follow.

The physical body is built around an energy template that tells each component of the body where it is to be located. When a soul wishes to take on a human body, it approaches the mass consciousness and asks for a copy of the template. The soul then uses this 'etheric' template to form the physical tissues around. At the end of May 2000, the human template was changed to incorporate these new chakra colours. This means that no one can take on human form without being able to 'fit' into the new phase one chakra colours. In July 2001, the template was further changed to incorporate the totally transparent chakra energies. As we progress through these changes, the etheric template will be further changed to suit the changed form and colours of the chakras. The end of September 2002 was the time when the template was changed to the third phase condition, that is, no chakras at all.

Earth Changes

In frequency terms, the chakras are also changed. Colour is only a function of frequency. The planet had its own energy 'signature' which began at 7.56 cycles per second. The red of the old chakra colours also began its frequency range at 7.56 cycles per second. All physical life on the planet also resonated with this frequency. The first chakra contains the energies of the first three dimensions and it is these energies which give us our physical form. As we travel through our own changes, the planet has altered to suit.

Part of the problem of being human is that this base frequency is too low. The energies contained within the soul are immense and slowing the base frequencies to the 7.56

174

level was a major component in humanity's demise. With this process of change well underway, the planet has also changed its base frequency from 7.56 to 3 500 cycles per second. This change also took place at the end of May 2000. This has allowed us to raise the base frequency of the first chakra to suit.

With the old colours, the frequency range for the human chakras was 7.56 cycles per second at their lowest to about 75 000 for the crown chakra. With these changes, the first begins at 3 500 cycles per second and the crown rises to in excess of 225 000 cycles per second.

Another way of measuring energy is by dimensions. A dimension can be defined as a marker point along a range of energy frequencies that incorporates above the last dimensional marker but below the next. With the old colours, the first chakra contained three dimensions whilst the total energy within the physical body contained a total of twelve dimensions. These new energy changes mean that the first will still contain the first three and the crown a minimum of forty two dimensions.

Physical and Emotional Symptoms

As with all periods of transition, problems can occur. Not all of the symptoms of change are comfortable.

One of the first signs of change that most notice is a headache. There are four psychic centres within the brain. These are located just above and behind the ear and at the base of the rear brain lobes. There are one of each on each side of the brain.

The human race is the only species in the whole universe who needs to communicate by speech. All other races communicate psychically. With our fall into the physical depths, we developed ways of communicating in a purely physical way and the psychic communication centres fell into disuse. As we begin our climb back to full consciousness, these centres need to be reawakened and they begin to expand.

To allow for expansion, the bones of the skull have to move very slightly and it is this skull plate movement which causes the headaches. The skull is made up of thirty two bones and by the time you reach the age of thirty, these bones can become fairly fixed. The internal pressure from the psychic centres means that all of the plates need to move together but usually cannot. This results in enormous pressure inside the head which can manifest itself as headaches, tooth ache for no apparent reason which can randomly move around the jaw, jaw ache and tension down the back of the neck and shoulders.

The only effective way of easing these pains is to consult a cranial osteopath or some one who can give a head massage. They do ultimately pass but they can be extremely painful whilst they last.

There can also be a tendency to delve into the past and question actions taken and their outcome. This is part of the DNA clearance process. It is impossible to be impassive in this process. Illness arises because we have gone against the wishes of the soul and these transgressions are transmitted through the chakras and into the appropriate organs of the body. In the past, we could ignore these promptings and forty years down the line, we would die of one illness or another. With the change of energies, communication between the soul and the body becomes immediate. Holding on to these past situations and the emotions that go with them will lead to the rapid onset of illness. There is nowhere to hide from the soul any more and all of these issues must be dealt with and cleared (for a full explanation of the relationship between the consciousness, the chakras, the body's organs and illnesses,

176

see Everything You Always Wanted To Know About Your Body But, So Far, Nobody's Been Able To tell You by Chris Thomas and Diane Baker).

The same applies to relationships. We can put up with unacceptable behaviour within a relationship for some time by closing our mind to it. As with past issues, these problems can no longer be ignored. Relationship problems must be resolved or severe illness will arise very quickly. If they cannot be resolved, the relationship must be ended.

One of the symptoms of change is the sense of tension within the body, leading to high stress levels. This symptom comes about because there is a sense of something going on but not being able to identify it. The answer to this is we are changing and all that we can do, once we have begun the process, is to go with it. We cannot accelerate our progress through these changes as we are changing at a rate to suit us personally. But, if we try to fight these changes, we can slow their progress down and prolong the problems. Some are finding an increased need for sleep and feel tired even following minor exertion. The body's organs and processes are changing. As they change all of the body's systems need time to adjust. The ones which take longest to adjust are the immune system, the endocrine system and the lymphatic system. The endocrine system in particular can be a problem.

The endocrine is the body's hormone system. Hormones pass messages around the body to keep the organs etc functioning correctly. There are dozens of hormones in the body so keeping them in balance has always been a potential problem. With the processes of the body now speeding up, the hormones are put to greater use and if there is any imbalance in the system, the messages can take longer to arrive, putting stress within the body sometimes leading to bouts of depression for no apparent reason but especially tiredness.

There are many other symptoms which appear on an individual basis. The ones listed here are the main ones. Other symptoms are usually a variation on these.

Knowing the Truth

As we progress through these changes, there is a growing realisation that we are more than we thought we were. Somehow a space seems to open somewhere which makes us think that we have been living with only a small part of ourselves attached. As the higher self becomes more and more easily accessible, the speed at which answers arrive increases. The more we question, the more we seem to receive answers.
In the past we have relied on Gurus, Avatars, priests, etc to lead us to some answers. The more we realise that we have all of the answers to any of the questions we might ask contained within ourselves the more we begin to realise that a guru is not necessary.

Our search for answers, in the past, has quite often led us into the clutches of unscrupulous so called teachers and many problems have arisen. There is a new 'meritrea', 'he' is contained within each and every one us, the soul. We no longer need to look outside of ourselves to find the answers we need for our lives. They are already available, we just have to ask.

There is a growing body of people who reject authority. Politicians, doctors, scientists, priests, industrialists, bankers, governments, etc no longer hold any answers and the falseness of their activities no longer fool us into believing that they have any answers. Along with change comes the truth and an unwillingness to accept anything other than the truth. Where falsehood exists, it is spotted immediately as only the truth resonates with the body.

178

The same is true for our day to day dealings with friends, family and colleagues. We begin to find that we can only respond to situations with total honesty and can only accept total honesty in return. Anything else does not fit.

Ancient Energies and Ancient Promises

In addition to these physical changes within the body, these huge shifts in energy patterns are bringing problems to the surface which have previously remained hidden, sometimes since the very early days of Atlantis. As a "psychic surgeon", the author has an ability to track the energies of problems within the body back to their root cause. Ninety five percent of all illnesses relate to problems arising during this current life time. Illness arises because we have moved against the direct wishes of the consciousness and have depleted the energies of one or more chakras. With the chakra out of balance, an associated organ becomes affected and an illness arises. If we take steps to undo that imbalance, correct our wandering behaviour, the chakra returns to balance and the illness disappears of its own accord.

To achieve the third phase of the changes discussed above, we must have realised the connection between the consciousness and illness and corrected our behaviour to set ourselves upon 'the right path'. However, with these changes, there are those who have made all of the right moves, corrected all of the imbalances within their lives and still find that their health problem will not go away. In these instances, it is a fair indicator that we are talking about one of the more unusual causes brought about by these energy integration processes.
It must be stressed that such conditions are extremely rare. Ninety five percent of all illnesses relate to imbalances within this lifetime. Of the other five percent, the bulk will be made up of past life or multidimensional integration problems. Only about one half of one percent of health problems arise because of conditions brought about by the following causes.

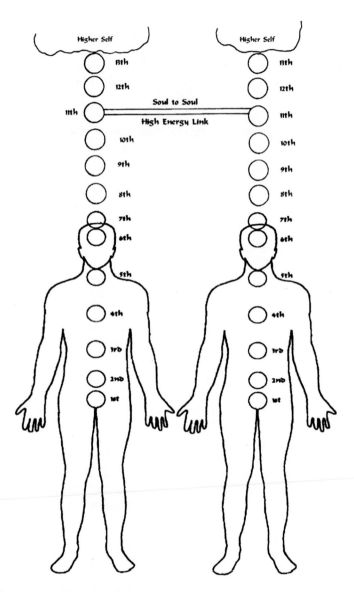

Illustration Number Four
'Linked Souls'

180

Links

Apart from the First Born of Earth, everyone has come to Earth from somewhere other. The vast majority of souls who came to Earth are from the six non physical civilisations. These are souls who exist in a purely energetic form i.e. they do not have any physical density. In coming to Atlantis, they would experience physical density for the very first time. Many were a little apprehensive about this new way of being and so two, or more, souls could promise to each other that they would help share any difficulties. If the promise of assistance was powerful enough, the souls became "linked".

The same applied if someone from the seven semi physical civilisations came to Earth. As these beings exist in a semi physical state, the transition to full physical density was not such a big step and so were more able to deal with life as a human. If, however, they encountered someone from the six who were experiencing difficulties, they could offer assistance and a similar "link" would form.

These links meant that the souls connected in this way could share their experiences and portion problem areas between the souls connected. As we began to lose our higher capabilities as Atlantis progressed, we forgot about these links and the two souls have remained linked together ever since. This means that during subsequent lifetimes, if the two people linked in this way shared a lifetime, whether together in a family group or even if they were thousands of miles apart, the one who offered to take on the problems of the other has done just that. This means that if one person within the linked pair had difficulties with aspects of their lives, they could offload those difficulties down the link and into the person they were linked to.

In previous lifetimes these links have not presented too major a set of problems but in this lifetime, they are disastrous. Firstly, it means that if you are clearing all of your issues and bringing yourself back into full balance, there remain issues and problems which do not belong to you and, given our much greater physical density, they become impossible to clear. Where such links do exist, the problems received from the other person are stored down the left side of the body. Another common symptom is to feel panicky on waking in the morning and the feelings of panic diminish during the day. The feelings of panic arise because at some level you recognise that you have a problem that is beyond the norm and one which is difficult to rectify.

An additional problem associated with links is that as you progress through these changes, the link acts like a knot in the higher energies making it very difficult for you to draw down the higher energies into the body.

If you suspect that you have one of these links, about the only way of dealing with it is to ask your higher self to contact a 'guide' who has the energy potential to cut the link.

Chips

We mentioned the use of diamond shaped energy genetic accelerators in chapter three. These were used to accelerate the development of cro magnon man into homo sapien. These energy matrices were also used by those on Atlantis to alter their physical form and this led, eventually, to many bizarre experiments taking place. This was not the only use to which these energy 'chips' were put. Where the use of a chip was made to alter something comparatively straight forward such as skin texture, they were not a problem and many of those who made use of them for such purposes retained them. They have not been a problem during subsequent life times but, with our now taking on board the higher energies of the higher self, many of these Atlantean chips are being reactivated and strange physical alterations are beginning to occur.

Another use for these chips was at the end of Atlantis, when it was known that the continent needed to be destroyed, a number of people made use of these chips to give themselves a better chance of surviving the destruction and to give them a greater chance of survival on the post Atlantis Earth. It is chips used mainly for this purpose that are causing the greatest problems.

Most of these chips have become degraded over the intervening lifetimes and so do not carry any specific genetic sequencing but they are causing disruption to the smooth flow of energy within the body.

The chips are always located on the spine, just above the heart chakra. The reason for locating them there is that the heart chakra is the chakra which the higher self uses to communicate to the physical body. The process it uses is the endocrine system which is controlled by this chakra. By locating the chips here, the body's messenger system, the endocrine, is easily accessed.

Case Histories

The best way of illustrating these kinds of problems is to draw upon case histories from the author's psychic surgery practice. The kinds of problems these chips can create are quite diverse and some can be quite drastic in the alterations being made to the body. For example, various animal forms have very advanced survival tools and it is these characteristics which the chip contains.

Some people have reported immensely slow digestive systems and they have experienced very little appetite for food. The symptoms suddenly began about five or six years ago. These are symptomatic of a chip within their systems containing snake genes. Snakes only need to eat about every three months and so require very little in the way of food. As a

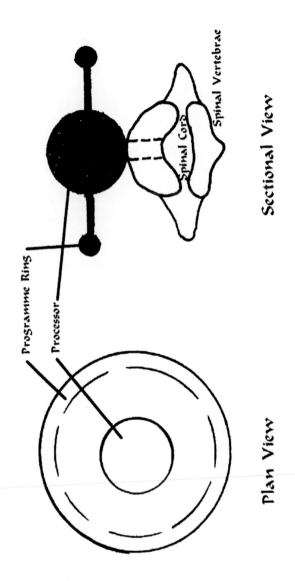

Spinal Vertebrae

Spinal Cord

Programme Ring

Processor

Sectional View

Plan View

Illustration Number 5
An NGC 'Galaxy Chip

184

survival tool, it is perfect, as if you are entering an unfamiliar world, how do you know where your next meal is coming from?

The author's personal favourite is one encountered in four different people. The symptoms were of the pelvis beginning to curl inwards bringing the knees together with a gradual loss of the ability to walk comfortably. Two of these clients were experiencing major changes to their hearing and could not tolerate any kind of music or noise even at quite gentle levels. One client had a bony growth surgically removed from her spine some time before seeing her. Their chips carried gene sequences which were turning them into mermaids. The curl to the pelvis and loss of leg function were the pelvis and legs turning into the fish tail. The hearing problems came about because they were developing gill chambers behind the ear and the bony growth was a fin beginning to grow.

Bizarre as these seem, they were very real problems experienced by these clients.

Galaxy Chips

This is another type of chip entirely different in their form and function to the Atlantean chips described above. These chips were developed by the semi physical race we know as NGC 584.

In their work as the universe's 'master geneticists' the NGC need to be able to move freely between dimensional space. Every region of the universe has differing energy structures and so travel to each region requires an ability to cross dimensions. The primary function of these kinds of chips is to make this form of travel possible. Not too many humans require this ability just at the moment and so this function is dormant. However, these chips have several other functions and it is these functions that are currently causing problems.

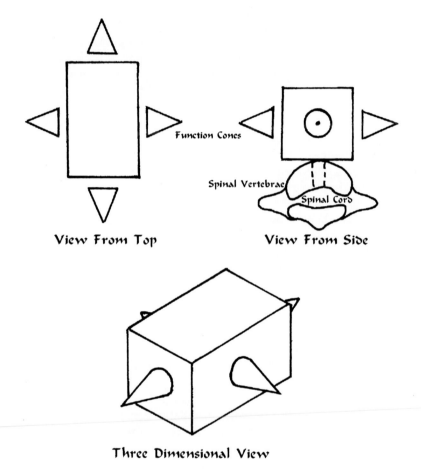

View From Top

View From Side

Function Cones

Spinal Vertebrae

Spinal Cord

Three Dimensional View

Illustration Number Six
An "Updated" Galaxy Chip

These chips are also located on the spine, just above the heart chakra. They are circular in form with the outer ring carrying programme information. The central 'lump' is an information processor and all of the body's nerves connect into it. The processor acts a little like the brain's hypothalamus, processing all of the information coming in from the nervous system, the programme segments then modify functions within the body depending upon the nerve impulses picked up by the processor.

There are several types of problems arising from these chips. The most common problem is an aspect of the dimensional space function. It is possible to connect several people together so that the whole group can travel en masse through the dimensional barriers. This connecting ability forms links to other souls and many of the problems described for soul links described above can occur. Another problem is that if you experience a particularly emotional period, the chip remembers the experience and can hold the effects of the trauma within the organ affected causing dysfunction within the organ that are very difficult to clear.

The strongest affect comes about because of one the chip's other primary functions. Unlike human geneticists, the NGC act with extreme integrity in all of the work they do. The primary role the NGC have taken on is to assist developing planets with the introduction of plant or animal species chosen by the planet's consciousness for particular roles on that world. Say, for example, a new planet wants to have grass growing on its surface. The NGC will travel to Earth and borrow the etheric template for grass from the Earth's consciousness. They will then make the necessary alterations, energetic and genetic, to the grass and trigger a function of the chip. This function allows the NGC to wrap themselves in an energy field which allows them to travel through time and dimensional space to ensure that the modifications are correct and there are no faults within the modifications. They then

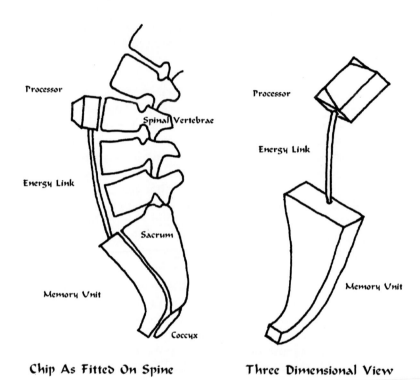

Processor

Spinal Vertebrae

Energy Link

Sacrum

Memory Unit

Coccyx

Chip As Fitted On Spine

Processor

Energy Link

Memory Unit

Three Dimensional View

Illustration Number Seven
A 'Sirian' Chip

return to current time and space knowing that the new plant will not cause any problems on the new world. In human terms, this enveloping field function can be switched on if the person with the chip feels threatened. It can generate a kind of defensive barrier around the body. Unfortunately, with this barrier in place, not only does it shut you away from the world making it difficult to interact with others easily, the barrier also holds emotional trauma in place within the aura making it almost impossible to clear emotional issues.

The 'updated' version of the chip has also been found in animals. In these instances, the chip has been placed to enhance communication between the animal and its owner.

Sirian Chips

These are again, totally different in form and structure to the other two types of chip carried by some people (see illustration). These chips sit on the lower spine with the triangular piece covering the sacrum and coccyx.

The 'lozenge' shaped piece acts as a kind of processor with the sacrum section acting as a memory store. They were designed by the Sirians as memory recorders to supplement the loss of eleven DNA spirals when we first embarked on the human plan.

But, not only do they remember, they also recycle those memories. Memories also include emotional events or events which resulted in physical damage to the body. Say, for example, you fell over and broke your wrist. The chip picks up on the event but then sees the broken bone as now being part of the body's natural structure. This makes the bone very slow to heal and even when it does, the shock and pain of the injury can remain locked within the wrist making it always uncomfortable.

People with these kinds of chip can also experience the mental reliving of events replayed within their heads as an almost constant cycle making it very difficult to clear memories. Ideas can also be recycled in this way making the person embroider many other occurrences around the original idea or event memory leading to accusations of living in a fantasy world.

It must be remembered that these kinds of chips are extremely rare and they were voluntarily placed into the body by the person carrying them. These chips have not been imposed upon the individual but were chosen to perform a particular function at a particular time in that person's past. Some were taken on in Atlantean times, approximately 70 000 years ago, whilst some are even older than that.

Other energy matrices found in people's bodies are chips built in Sumerian times, 15 000 years ago. These are similar to Atlantean chips but are sixteen pointed instead of six. Shamanic healers can sometimes create energy structures to assist their client's healing. These are usually three sided versions of the Atlantean chips and also have a 'barbed' hook type aspect to 'hook' the chip into the client's spinal energy flow. These can also be used by unscrupulous shamanic healers to control the energy flow within the body.

Crystal healers can also create permanent energy matrices connected onto the spine. The ones created by crystal healers usually have the form and function of a double terminated quartz crystal. These are usually attached to the client to allow the healing work to continue for a long period of time after the healing session.

One thing all of these chips, barbs and crystals have in common: they ultimately disturb and disrupt the smooth flow of energy up and down the spine, making the higher self integration process very difficult to achieve.

Adding the chip into the body in the first place was an act of free choice and so the removal of the chip requires an equal act of choice.

The best way to remove these chips is to work with the higher self and ask that it contacts someone, physical or non physical, who is able to remove the chip from your system and can counteract the energetic, physical or genetic effects these chips can have.

The Legacy of the Fourteenth Faction

The Fourteenth Faction and their affect on Universal history and activity was discussed in Chapter Ten. As well as effectively destroying about one third of the Universes' resources, they have also generated energy forms within some peoples' bodies and 'booby trapped' some areas of the Universe. These energy forms are continuing to be active and have the potential to disrupt.

These chips and devices were not taken on voluntarily, they were forcibly imposed by the Fourteen either on the individual who carries them or into the regions of space where the 'booby' trap devices remain.

The purpose of the 'communicator' was to collect all energies from any energy source, be that human, animal, plant, or the Earth. The energies were gathered by the crystal located in the abdomen, transferred and stored in the battery pack and, at an appropriate time, transmitted through the throat communicator to a central storage facility or directly to the Fourteen's home universe (see below). The duplicator chip located on the sacrum was used to replicate the whole device should it be removed. Several people on Earth still carry these devices and they can disrupt the energy flows within the body particularly within the abdomen and the throat there is also, usually, a sense of some kind of disruption taking place within the region of the sacrum. Remember that these devices are made of energy frequencies that are not of this Universe and are incompatible with the energies of the human body and so can cause major disruption to the body's structures.

These devices are, fortunately, exceptionally rare. The Akashic records that 124 people, on Earth, have these devices fitted and at least 90 have been removed and destroyed. The remainder are in individuals who have chosen to make use of their potential, the heads of some of the transnational companies.

The other device is entirely different. These devices are empty shells of energy. The fact that they are completely empty is in itself something of an anomaly. There cannot be a state of nothing within this universe. Although there appear to be regions where 'nothing' exists, there is always energies of some kind. With these devices there is absolutely nothing within the outside shell. No energy, no substance, nothing, a complete abomination.

The purpose of the Fourteen entering this universe was to plunder its resources. In order to do this they constructed these 'booby' traps. The booby traps were an enigma about which many were curious. When touched, the traps imploded, drawing in the energy of the soul and using it to construct a 'worm hole' into the Fourteen's universe. As the worm hole formed, it would draw into it all of the energies around the region be that star, planet or individual. In all, 984 souls were destroyed by these devices and many more were drawn through the worm hole into the other universe to an unknown future. Many of those caught in the blast were severely harmed and irreparably damaged on a soul level. As a worm hole formed, the communicator devices would discharge their battery packs and an energy surge would pass from this universe into the other. Using these devices, the Fourteen have destroyed about one third of this universes' resources.

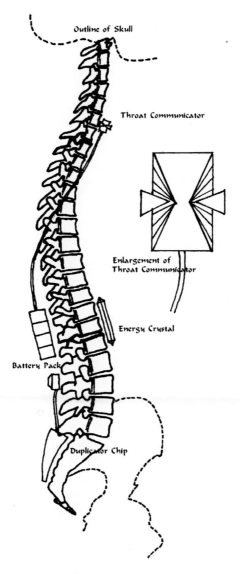

Illustration Number Eight
A Fourteen 'Communicator'

There are a number of these booby trap soul destroyers still within the universe but all have been marked and no one approaches them.

Many have asked how could events and humanity's actions on Earth have been allowed to decline so far. This is the answer. Those who would have come to our aid and gently steer us back onto the right course were caught upin a battle for the survival of the universe and of necessity humanity was left to fend for itself. Earth was deliberately isolated away from the universe in an attempt to keep it safe from the Fourteen. Even Merlin was deliberately kept unaware of these events until the 'war' was almost won.

Future Solutions

So, what of the future, where are these changes taking us?

An aspect of this waking up process is that many people are saying that they feel as though 'they have a job to do' and they are here for a purpose. It is true.

Everyone who is physical at this time is here to complete a job they began some time ago or they are here to begin a job they have undertaken to complete when humanity has woken up. Regardless of the damage humanity has wreaked upon this planet, if humanity was removed tomorrow, the planet would be back to its pristine condition within fifty thousand years. On this time frame, humanity would not have existed. If the threat of GM is removed, the planet will recover. However, we live on a planet where humans have created a great deal of damage and it is the responsibility of humanity to clean it up. As was stated in an earlier chapter, mankind cannot undo the damage, or potential damage, that GM organisms are capable of doing to the planet, only the Sidhé are capable of that, but the overall damage really is our responsibility.

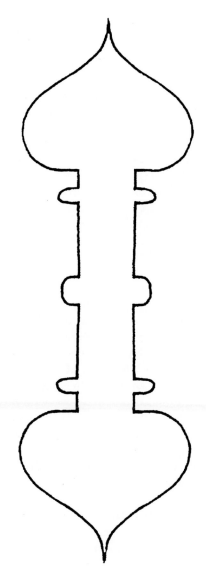

Illustration Number Nine
A Fourteen 'Booby' Trap Device

Twenty thousand years ago, when we returned to the planet following the Atlantis destruction, we had all of the consciousness within the physical body. Our capabilities were considerably beyond anything we have experienced since. As an example, Stonehenge was built 10 000 years ago using our inherent telekinetic capability. Merlin 'rode' the blue stones from the Preseli Mountains in Pembrokeshire to Salisbury Plain and then erected the stones by telekinesis. The pyramids of Egypt were built in the same way, as were many of the older structures in South America. Both the Egyptian and South American structures were actually built around eighteen thousand years ago. The same principles of building are still used in some parts of Tibet and Outer Mongolia today by Buddhist priests to build their monasteries. If we collect a group of like minded individuals together and produce a resonant sound, we can literally move mountains.

The original time frame we set ourselves to complete The Human Plan was by the end of 2011. Given the threat of GM and some of the problems generated by those who have taken on and acted with the energies of the Fourteen, by common consent, Merlin has accelerated the energies necessary to complete these changes to the end of 2005. This means that all of those who made their choice to complete The Plan must have done so by the end of 2005. Those who have chosen not to complete The Plan must leave the planet by the end of 2005. If we do not fulfil our promise and potential by the end of 2005, the Earth will no longer make itself available to us and by the end of 2011 no human life will remain on Earth apart from the First Born.

We are now undergoing the process of returning to us, the us of the total soul. The us who understands the universe. The us who first arrived on this planet 85 000 years ago. The us who will inherit this Earth. Those who built Stonehenge, those who built the Pyramids are here once again. As we become whole, those skills return. Those understandings return and the damage we have created on this planet in the last seven thousand years can be undone. The Russians have already proven that nuclear waste can be neutralised by psychic processes and this is before we complete our integration!

This is what our job is. This is what we are all here to do at this time. We are here to complete The Human Plan and we are here to undo the damage done by man. If we can avoid the horrendous threat of GM we can undo our harm. All are armed and ready to carry out this work and we will prevail.

There is little point in attempting this work until we have finished our transition. Ninety nine percent of the work carried out by groups wishing to 'heal the planet' carried out during the day is undone by those who work by night when the consciousness leaves the body and has full knowledge of their actions. It is pointless trying to prevent the planet relieve its own stresses by attempting to divert or prevent earthquakes as all that does is increase the magnitude of those that do occur. Instead of avoiding your own issues by 'healing the planet', accept your own changes and transitions as they arise and we might actually save this planet from what we have done to it. Interfere and all is lost.

The planet is a consciousness that is undergoing its own consciousness changes. In the same way as we are experiencing 'growing pains', so is the planet. It must be allowed to act freely and in ways in which it sees fit. Preventing the release of inner stresses (earthquakes and volcanoes) brought about by the planet's own growth can, and does, only cause damage and the whole process of our positive change disrupted.

We can do nothing positive until we have finished our awakening. When we have awoken, we will know. All else is ego.

Appendix Two

Earth Chronology

347 million Years Ago	solar system completed with all thirteen planets established and the energy envelope complete
40 million Years Ago forms began on the	establishment of the first life outer planets
20.5 million Years Ago	life began on Earth
20 million Years Ago	creation of the Sidhé and the Faerie
4.5 million Years Ago	Neanderthal Man stepped out from the primates
4 million Years Ago	arrival of Merlin on Earth
3.9 million Years Ago	removal of four planets from the solar system
3.8 Million Years Ago	Cro Magnon Man arrives from Mars
1 Million Years Ago	end of the last Ice Age
94-88 Thousand Years Ago	period when Lemuria was established

85 000 Years Ago	Atlantis established
70 000 Years Ago	Atlantis destroyed
28 000 Years Ago	human energy matrix established
20 000 Years Ago	human resettlement begun
7 000 Years Ago	beginnings of The Human Plan, Karma

1996	primary energy matrix energised. Each person assessed their own readiness to complete the consciousness integration process
2005 (end of)	the accelerated completion date for human consciousness integration
2011	last and absolutely final date for the completion of the consciousness integration process

FREE DETAILED CATALOGUE

Capall Bann is owned and run by people actively involved in many of the areas in which we publish. A detailed illustrated catalogue is available on request, SAE or International Postal Coupon appreciated. **Titles can be ordered direct from Capall Bann, post free in the UK** (cheque or PO with order) or from good bookshops and specialist outlets.

Do contact us for details on the latest releases at: **Capall Bann Publishing, Auton Farm, Milverton, Somerset, TA4 1NE.** Titles include:

A Breath Behind Time, Terri Hector
Angels and Goddesses - Celtic Christianity & Paganism, M. Howard
Astrology The Inner Eye - A Guide in Everyday Language, E Smith
Auguries and Omens - The Magical Lore of Birds, Yvonne Aburrow
Asyniur - Womens Mysteries in the Northern Tradition, S McGrath
Between Earth and Sky, Julia Day
Book of the Veil , Peter Paddon
Caer Sidhe - Celtic Astrology and Astronomy, Michael Bayley
Call of the Horned Piper, Nigel Jackson
Cat's Company, Ann Walker
Celtic Faery Shamanism, Catrin James
Celtic Faery Shamanism - The Wisdom of the Otherworld, Catrin James
Celtic Lore & Druidic Ritual, Rhiannon Ryall
Celtic Sacrifice - Pre Christian Ritual & Religion, Marion Pearce
Celtic Saints and the Glastonbury Zodiac, Mary Caine
Circle and the Square, Jack Gale
Compleat Vampyre - The Vampyre Shaman, Nigel Jackson
Creating Form From the Mist - The Wisdom of Women in Celtic Myth and
     Culture, Lynne Sinclair-Wood
Crystal Clear - A Guide to Quartz Crystal, Jennifer Dent
Crystal Doorways, Simon & Sue Lilly
Dragons of the West, Nigel Pennick
Earth Dance - A Year of Pagan Rituals, Jan Brodie
Earth Harmony - Places of Power, Holiness & Healing, Nigel Pennick
Earth Magic, Margaret McArthur
Eildon Tree (The) Romany Language & Lore, Michael Hoadley
Enchanted Forest - The Magical Lore of Trees, Yvonne Aburrow
Eternal Priestess, Sage Weston
Eternally Yours Faithfully, Roy Radford & Evelyn Gregory
Everything You Always Wanted To Know About Your Body, But So Far
     Nobody's Been Able To Tell You, Chris Thomas & D Baker

Face of the Deep - Healing Body & Soul, Penny Allen
Fairies in the Irish Tradition, Molly Gowen
Familiars - Animal Powers of Britain, Anna Franklin
Fool's First Steps, (The) Chris Thomas
Forest Paths - Tree Divination, Brian Harrison, Ill. S. Rouse
From Past to Future Life, Dr Roger Webber
God Year, The, Nigel Pennick & Helen Field
Goddess Year, The, Nigel Pennick & Helen Field
Goddesses, Guardians & Groves, Jack Gale
Handbook For Pagan Healers, Liz Joan
Handbook of Fairies, Ronan Coghlan
Healing Book, The, Chris Thomas and Diane Baker
Healing Homes, Jennifer Dent
Healing Journeys, Paul Williamson
Healing Stones, Sue Philips
Herb Craft - Shamanic & Ritual Use of Herbs, Lavender & Franklin
Hidden Heritage - Exploring Ancient Essex, Terry Johnson
Hub of the Wheel, Skytoucher
In Search of Herne the Hunter, Eric Fitch
Inner Space Workbook - Develop Thru Tarot, C Summers & J Vayne
Intuitive Journey, Ann Walker Isis - African Queen, Akkadia Ford
Journey Home, The, Chris Thomas
Kecks, Keddles & Kesh - Celtic Lang & The Cog Almanac, Bayley
Legend of Robin Hood, The, Richard Rutherford-Moore
Lid Off the Cauldron, Patricia Crowther
Light From the Shadows - Modern Traditional Witchcraft, Gwyn
Living Tarot, Ann Walker
Lore of the Sacred Horse, Marion Davies
Lost Lands & Sunken Cities (2nd ed.), Nigel Pennick
Magic of Herbs - A Complete Home Herbal, Rhiannon Ryall
Magical Guardians - Exploring the Spirit and Nature of Trees, Philip Heselton
Magical History of the Horse, Janet Farrar & Virginia Russell
Magical Lore of Animals, Yvonne Aburrow
Magical Lore of Cats, Marion Davies
Magical Lore of Herbs, Marion Davies
Masks of Misrule - Horned God & His Cult in Europe, Nigel Jackson
Medicine For The Coming Age, Lisa Sand MD
Medium Rare - Reminiscences of a Clairvoyant, Muriel Renard
Mind Massage - 60 Creative Visualisations, Marlene Maundrill
Mirrors of Magic - Evoking the Spirit of the Dewponds, P Heselton
Moon Mysteries, Jan Brodie
Mysteries of the Runes, Michael Howard
Mystic Life of Animals, Ann Walker
Oracle of Geomancy, Nigel Pennick
Pagan Feasts - Seasonal Food for the 8 Festivals, Franklin & Phillips
Patchwork of Magic - Living in a Pagan World, Julia Day

Pathworking - A Practical Book of Guided Meditations, Pete Jennings
Personal Power, Anna Franklin
Pillars of Tubal Cain, Nigel Jackson
Places of Pilgrimage and Healing, Adrian Cooper
Practical Meditation, Steve Hounsome
Psychic Self Defence - Real Solutions, Jan Brodie
Real Fairies, David Tame
Reality - How It Works & Why It Mostly Doesn't, Rik Dent
Romany Tapestry, Michael Houghton
Runic Astrology, Nigel Pennick
Sacred Animals, Gordon MacLellan
Sacred Celtic Animals, Marion Davies, Ill. Simon Rouse
Sacred Grove - The Mysteries of the Forest, Yvonne Aburrow
Sacred Geometry, Nigel Pennick
Sacred Nature, Ancient Wisdom & Modern Meanings, A Cooper
Sacred Ring - Pagan Origins of British Folk Festivals, M. Howard
Season of Sorcery - On Becoming a Wisewoman, Poppy Palin
Seasonal Magic - Diary of a Village Witch, Paddy Slade
Secret Places of the Goddess, Philip Heselton
Secret Signs & Sigils, Nigel Pennick
Self Enlightenment, Mayan O'Brien
Spirits of the Earth sereis, Jaq D Hawkins
Stumbling Through the Undergrowth , Mark Kirwan-Heyhoe
Subterranean Kingdom, The, revised 2nd ed, Nigel Pennick
Talking to the Earth, Gordon MacLellan
Taming the Wolf - Full Moon Meditations, Steve Hounsome
The Other Kingdoms Speak, Helena Hawley
Tree: Essence of Healing, Simon & Sue Lilly
Vortex - The End of History, Mary Russell
Warriors at the Edge of Time, Jan Fry
Way of the Magus, Michael Howard
Weaving a Web of Magic, Rhiannon Ryall
West Country Wicca, Rhiannon Ryall
Wildwood King , Philip Kane
Wondrous Land - The Faery Faith of Ireland by Dr Kay Mullin
Working With the Merlin, Geoff Hughes

FREE detailed catalogue and FREE 'Inspiration' magazine

Contact: Capall Bann Publishing, Auton Farm, Milverton, Somerset, TA4 1NE